Learning Centers for
School Libraries

AASL Standards-Based Learning

Learning Centers
for School Libraries

Maura Madigan

ALA Editions

CHICAGO | 2021

American Association
of School Librarians

TRANSFORMING LEARNING

Maura Madigan is a school librarian in Fairfax County, Virginia. She's worked in education for twenty-five years in the United States, South Korea, Japan, and the United Arab Emirates, including two years on a school reform project for the Abu Dhabi Education Council. Maura often presents on learning centers and problem-based learning at conferences. Her work has appeared in *School Library Journal, The Travel 100, Oasis Living Magazine,* and *Effective School Librarianship: Successful Professional Practices from Librarians around the World.*

Extensive effort has gone into ensuring the reliability of the information in this book; however, the publisher makes no warranty, express or implied, with respect to the material contained herein.

ISBN: 978-0-8389-4973-3 (paper)

Library of Congress Cataloging-in-Publication Data
Names: Madigan, Maura, 1969- author.
Title: Learning centers for school libraries / Maura Madigan.
Description: Chicago : ALA Editions, 2021. | Series: AASL standards-based learning | Includes bibliographical references and index. | Summary: "Learning Centers for School Libraries contains detailed, step-by-step instructions and reproducible templates for over 20 learning centers"— Provided by publisher.
Identifiers: LCCN 2020045657 | ISBN 9780838949733 (paperback)
Subjects: LCSH: School libraries—Activity programs—United States. | School libraries—Activity programs—United States—Case studies. | Instructional materials centers—Activity programs— United States. | Instructional materials centers—Activity programs—United States—Case studies. | Library orientation for school children—United States.
Classification: LCC Z675.S3 M214 2021 | DDC 027.8—dc23
LC record available at https://lccn.loc.gov/2020045657

Composition by Alejandra Diaz in the Utopia Std and Galano Classic typefaces.

☉ This paper meets the requirements of ANSI/NISO Z39.48-1992 (Permanence of Paper).

Printed in the United States of America
25 24 23 22 21   5 4 3 2 1

For my father,
JAMES BOWEN,
who always said I should write a book.

CONTENTS

ACKNOWLEDGMENTS

I wrote this book during the COVID-19 quarantine. It felt a bit odd writing a book about learning centers, many of which require hands-on participation and collaboration, during a time of social distancing. This book kept me focused and sane, picturing a time in the future when schools, libraries, and education would return to normal.

I have so many people to thank for their help with this book. First, my incredible editors, Stephanie Book and Jamie Santoro, for their excellent and timely feedback. It really was a joy to work with them.

Next, a huge thanks to Katie Bruechert, Fairfax County Public Schools (FCPS) librarian, who suggested I write this book. To all the FCPS librarians, teachers, and library support specialists past and present who continue to mentor and cheer me on: Marcie Atkins, Priscille Dando, Heather Jenkins, Valerie Jopeck, Jennifer Kalletta, Barbara McLeod, Suzie Miller, Terry Rihl, Kim Sigle, and Kesha Valentine. Thanks to Chad McRae, principal, and Leslie Malkowski, assistant principal, for their continued support, trust, and willingness to let me try new things.

To Ben Rudolph, master educator, for his Disruptus idea that morphed into my Innovation Station. To Tanya Parrott, Prince William County school librarian, for her many great ideas about using breakout boxes in the library. Her presentation at a Virginia Association of School Librarians conference was informative and extremely entertaining.

Finally, to my daughters—Annie, Kathleen, and Grace—for their patience and support and, most importantly, to my husband, Andrew, who's always been my biggest champion and best editor.

PREFACE

Creating Capable and Critical Minds

Whenever I read books, especially professional books, I'm always curious about the authors. Who are they, what's their background, and why should I trust them? When I present at conferences, participants often want to know about my school, my library, my schedule. This makes sense. They're trying to decide if my experience and ideas will work for them. So, here's some information about me. You may agree or disagree with my educational philosophy, but I hope you can find some common ground, enough to trust me and try learning centers for yourself.

I completed my fifth year as an elementary school librarian in 2020, but I have a total of twenty-five years in education. I've been a classroom teacher (preschool, kindergarten, second grade, sixth grade), a preschool director, a college instructor, and an educational advisor for an international school reform project. I've worked in public and private schools in several states and overseas. All these experiences have shaped the librarian I am today.

I endeavor to create a safe and inviting place so that a learner's first experience with the school library, books, and reading is a positive one. I think very carefully about my practices, constantly evaluating what I'm offering learners and what they need. I believe that elementary school librarians, because we regularly see every student in the school, have an incredible opportunity and a serious responsibility. We're able to roll out whole-school initiatives and help to even the playing field. I think about what essential skills are needed to be successful library patrons, researchers, and learners. Each year I've asked myself, "What can I provide that they aren't going to get from their classroom educator?" This question led me away from read-alouds. Yes, they are important, and fun, and yes, I do read books aloud in the school library, but most elementary classroom educators are already doing that.

During my first year as a school librarian, I was struggling with time management. I saw every class for thirty minutes a week. This thirty-minute class included checking out books and escorting learners to their next class. I had a really difficult time delivering meaningful lessons and making sure everyone was checked out, lined up, and ready to go on time. Larger classes often ended with one eye on the clock and the other frantically trying to zip through checkout. I was frazzled and disappointed that learners had such a rushed school library experience. I knew there had to be a better way.

I decided to experiment with learning centers in the school library. As a classroom educator, I'd used this structure with great success. I thought this approach just might solve my problems, and it did. I flipped the order and had learners check out books first. After checking out, they were free to choose a center. Learners could take as much time as they liked browsing the shelves and choosing books. I was free to help them find books and to make suggestions. As my schedule and class time changed, I adapted how and when I used learning centers.

It's not all learning centers all the time. They're just one part of my repertoire that also includes problem-based learning projects, Guided Inquiry Design projects, research lessons, book talks, and read-alouds. Mixing things up makes it fun for me and my learners. I'm always looking for ideas and activities, and each year I add a few new learning centers. I also rethink and phase out centers that were consistently less popular or not as educationally valuable. Reflection is as important for those creating the lessons as it is for those doing the learning.

The following quotation from Piaget sums up my educational philosophy and what I hope to encourage in all my learners. Although the gender term used is outdated, the sentiment endures. I've replaced the exclusive term *men* with the more inclusive *learners*.

> The principal goal of education is to create [learners] who are capable of doing new things, not simply of repeating what other generations have done—[learners] who are creative, inventive, and discoverers. The second goal of education is to form minds which can be critical, can verify, and not accept everything they are offered. (Piaget 1964, 5)

The world needs learners who can think for themselves and solve problems in creative ways, not blindly accept and regurgitate facts. A good school librarian and school library help learners develop these attributes.

REFERENCE

Piaget, Jean. 1964. "Development and Learning." In *Piaget Rediscovered,* edited by R. E. Ripple and V. N. Rockcastle. Ithaca, NY: Cornell University Press.

INTRODUCTION
How to Use This Book

You've bought the book. Now what? Whether you're a learning center novice who wants step-by-step instructions or a seasoned pro looking for some new ideas, *Learning Centers for School Libraries* is here to help. The book is separated into two parts. Part I includes introductory material—the *what* and the *why*. Part II is the *how*, detailed descriptions of each learning center with handouts and worksheets that are easy to photocopy and will help you get started right away. This book is meant as a guide with as much of the prep work as possible included. Everything you need, all in one place.

WHAT TO EXPECT

Chapter 1, "Learning Centers," explains what learning centers are, why they're so valuable, and how you can integrate them into your current school library instruction. This chapter includes research supporting the importance of play, academic choice, and resiliency in education. It also discusses how learning centers address the *AASL Standards Framework for Learners* within the *National School Library Standards for Learners, School Librarians, and School Libraries*. You can use this section to justify the educational value of learning centers to administrators or colleagues. Included for easy reference is a Learning Centers and Standards table (table I.1), with short descriptions of each center, applicable AASL Standards, and aligned content-area standards.

Chapter 2, "Logistics," provides all the basics needed to get learning centers up and running smoothly. Topics include space, time, materials, cleaning and storage of materials, rules and routines, assessment, sharing and preservation of work, collaboration, and troubleshooting. This chapter also lists suggested materials for different budgets. You will probably want to refer to this chapter if you have general questions about managing your centers.

Part II includes twenty-five learning centers, grouped according to their primary focus, in chapters 3–7. Many centers have elements that will allow them to fit in various categories. Appendix A contains suggestions for ten centers that require little explanation. Each chapter begins with an overview and touches on pertinent AASL Standards and commonalities among the centers. A common format throughout the centers in part II makes it easy to find important information.

Each learning center is a mini-chapter that begins with a brief description and points to consider. This introduction is followed by the objective, relevant AASL Standards, content areas addressed, lesson duration, materials, educator preparation, learner steps, modifications, and extensions. At the end of each mini-chapter you'll find learner directions along with all necessary worksheets (WS) and reproducible materials.

Many of the centers can easily be adapted for distance learning because they rely on materials often found at home. An asterisk (*) appears next to these titles in the Learning Centers and Standards table (table I.1). Suggestions for ways in which to adapt the centers appear in the Modifications section within the mini-chapters. Learners can share their work with the school librarian and other learners by posting pictures and images online.

Whether teaching online or in person, you can pick and choose which centers to use with learners. There's no need to work in order. It's often more interesting to have a variety of centers for learners to choose from. Consider selecting one or two centers from each chapter to introduce and offer at a time. Alternatively, offer only one type of learning center at a time and have learners cycle through them over a series of weeks. This approach works especially well with the maker and literacy centers.

AASL STANDARDS AND CONTENT-AREA STANDARDS

It can be overwhelming for any educator to be given a set of standards and expected to create lessons to teach them. This is one reason AASL has published the Shared Foundations Series and the AASL Standards-Based Learning Series. Both series provide school librarians with concrete and creative ways to address the AASL Standards.

Learning Centers for School Libraries, part of the AASL Standards-Based Learning Series, is no exception. This book shows how learning centers target each of the Shared Foundations and Domains in the *AASL Standards Framework for Learners.* Specific Learner Competencies are listed within each center mini-chapter. Content areas that align well for possible collaboration with other educators are also listed in each center, but the specific content-area standards are contained in the Learning Centers and Standards table (table I.1). You can use this table to quickly locate centers that target specific Learner Competencies in the AASL Standards and content-area standards from other sets of national learning standards. This table can also be helpful when you are trying to build collaborative relationships with content-area educators.

The following national standards sets for content areas have been used:

- Art: National Core Arts Standards
- English/Language Arts (ELA): NCTE/IRA Standards for the English/Language Arts
- Mathematics: NCTM Principles and Standards for School Mathematics
- Science: Next Generation Science Standards (NGSS)
- Social Studies: C3 Framework for Social Studies Standards
- Technology: ISTE Standards for Students

SOME FINAL WORDS

It doesn't really matter how and when you introduce various learning centers. After a while you'll know which are the most popular with your learners. These might be ones you offer consistently. You might also be inspired to create some centers of your own or adapt some presented here. Learning centers are doable, worthwhile, and, above all, fun. I hope the learners in your school library enjoy learning centers as much as mine do.

TABLE I.1

Learning Centers and Standards

This table provides a short description of each learning center and links applicable AASL and content-area standards. This list is not meant to be exhaustive. Only the most pertinent standards appear.

The following national standards sets for content areas have been used:

- Art: National Core Arts Standards
- English/Language Arts (ELA): NCTE/IRA Standards for the English Language Arts
- Mathematics: NCTM Principles and Standards for School Mathematics
- Science: Next Generation Science Standards (NGSS)
- Social Studies: C3 Framework for Social Studies Standards
- Technology: ISTE Standards for Students

Centers that can be modified for use during distance or online learning are marked with an asterisk (*). These centers use materials that most learners have at home.

TABLE I.1

Learning Centers and Standards

Learning Center	AASL Standards Framework for Learners	Content-Area Standards
Maker Challenge* Learners use recycled materials to build something described on a challenge card using only string or yarn to hold it together. Page 21	V.B.2. (Explore/Create): Learners construct new knowledge by persisting through self-directed pursuits by tinkering and making. V.D. (Explore/Grow): Learners develop through experience and reflection by: 1. Iteratively responding to challenges. 2. Recognizing capabilities and skills that can be developed, improved, and expanded.	Art: Anchor Standard 1. Generate and conceptualize artistic ideas and work. ELA: 5. Students employ a wide range of strategies as they write and use different writing process elements appropriately to communicate with different audiences for a variety of purposes. Science: Use tools and materials provided to design and build a device that solves a specific problem or a solution to a specific problem. (K-PS3-2) Technology: Innovative Designer 4d. Students exhibit a tolerance for ambiguity, perseverance and the capacity to work with open-ended problems.
Innovation Station* Learners mentally dismantle the objects pictured on cards and invent or innovate a product using materials from two or more of the objects. Page 27	I.A.2. (Inquire/Think): Learners display curiosity and initiative by recalling prior and background knowledge as context for new meaning. III.C.1. (Collaborate/Share): Learners work productively with others to solve problems by soliciting and responding to feedback from others. V.B.1. (Explore/Create): Learners construct new knowledge by problem-solving through cycles of design, implementation, and reflection. V.C.3. (Explore/Share): Learners engage with the learning community by collaboratively identifying innovative solutions to a challenge or problem.	Art: Anchor Standard 10. Synthesize and relate knowledge and personal experiences to make art. ELA: 4. Students adjust their use of spoken, written, and visual language (e.g., conventions, style, vocabulary) to communicate effectively with a variety of audiences and for different purposes. ELA: 5. Students employ a wide range of strategies as they write and use different writing process elements appropriately to communicate with different audiences for a variety of purposes. Science: Define a simple problem that can be solved through the development of a new or improved object or tool. (3-PS2-4) Technology: Innovative Designer 4d. Students exhibit a tolerance for ambiguity, perseverance and the capacity to work with open-ended problems.

Learning Center	AASL Standards Framework for Learners	Content-Area Standards

Simple Machines*
 	
Learners use recycled materials to build pieces of playground equipment that feature simple machines (pulley, screw, wheel and axle, wedge, lever, and inclined plane).
 	
Page 37
	V.B. (Explore/Create): Learners construct new knowledge by:
	  1. Problem solving through cycles of design, implementation, and reflection.
	  2. Persisting through self-directed pursuits by tinkering and making.
	
	V.C.3. (Explore/Share): Learners engage with the learning community by collaboratively identifying innovative solutions to a challenge or problem.
		ELA: 5. Students employ a wide range of strategies as they write and use different writing process elements appropriately to communicate with different audiences for a variety of purposes.
		
		Science: Develop a model using an analogy, example, or abstract representation to describe a scientific principle. (4-PS4-1)
		
		Define a simple problem that can be solved through the development of a new or improved object or tool. (3-PS2-4)
		
		Technology: Innovative Designer 4d. Students exhibit a tolerance for ambiguity, perseverance and the capacity to work with open-ended problems.

Matchbox Car Engineering
 	
Learners use Matchbox-style tracks and cars to test scientific concepts such as gravity and speed.
 	
Page 49
	I.C. (Inquire/Share): Learners adapt, communicate, and exchange learning products with others in a cycle that includes:
	  2. Providing constructive feedback.
	  3. Acting on feedback to improve.
	
	II.C. (Include/Share): Learners exhibit empathy with and tolerance for diverse ideas by:
	  1. Engaging in informed conversation and active debate.
	  2. Contributing to discussions in which multiple viewpoints on a topic are expressed.
	
	III.D. (Collaborate/Grow): Learners actively participate with others in learning situations by:
	  1. Actively contributing to group discussions.
	  2. Recognizing learning as a social responsibility.
	
	V.C.3. (Explore/Share): Learners engage with the learning community by collaboratively identifying innovative solutions to a challenge or problem.
		Math: Measurement: Apply appropriate techniques, tools, and formulas to determine measurements.
		
		Connections: Recognize and apply mathematics in contexts outside of mathematics.
		
		Science: Measure and graph quantities such as weight to address scientific and engineering questions and problems. (5-PS1-2)
		
		Develop a model using an example to describe a scientific principle. (5-ESS2-1)
		
		Make observations and/or measurements to produce data to serve as the basis for evidence for an explanation of a phenomenon or test a design solution. (3-PS2-2, 4-PS3-2, 4-ESS2-1, 5-PS1-3)

(cont'd)

TABLE I.1

Learning Centers and Standards (cont'd)

Learning Center	AASL Standards Framework for Learners	Content-Area Standards
Construction Learners explore their creativity while working on fine motor skills with a variety of materials. Page 56	V.B.2. (Explore/Create): Learners construct new knowledge by persisting through self-directed pursuits by tinkering and making. V.D.1. (Explore/Grow): Learners develop through experience and reflection by iteratively responding to challenges.	Art: Anchor Standard 1. Generate and conceptualize artistic ideas and work. ELA: 5. Students employ a wide range of strategies as they write and use different writing process elements appropriately to communicate with different audiences for a variety of purposes. Science: Use tools and materials provided to design and build a device that solves a specific problem or a solution to a specific problem. (K-PS3-2) Technology: Innovative Designer 4d. Students exhibit a tolerance for ambiguity, perseverance and the capacity to work with open-ended problems.
Fairy-Tale Challenge* Learners read a familiar fairy tale, identify the problem, and formulate possible solutions. Then they use recycled materials to complete a challenge based on the story. Page 60	V.A.1. (Explore/Think): Learners develop and satisfy personal curiosity by reading widely and deeply in multiple formats and write and create for a variety of purposes. V.B. (Explore/Create): Learners construct new knowledge by: 1. Problem solving through cycles of design, implementation, and reflection. 2. Persisting through self-directed pursuits by tinkering and making.	ELA: 3. Students apply a wide range of strategies to comprehend, interpret, evaluate, and appreciate texts. They draw on their prior experience, their interactions with other readers and writers, their knowledge of word meaning and of other texts, their word identification strategies, and their understanding of textual features (e.g., sound-letter correspondence, sentence structure, context, graphics). ELA: 5. Students employ a wide range of strategies as they write and use different writing process elements appropriately to communicate with different audiences for a variety of purposes. Science: Use tools and materials provided to design and build a device that solves a specific problem or a solution to a specific problem. (K-PS3-2)

Learning Center	AASL Standards Framework for Learners	Content-Area Standards
Mini Green Screen Learners use a tablet, pizza box, and a green screen app to create movies. Page 69	I.B.3. (Inquire/Create): Learners engage with new knowledge by following a process that includes generating products that illustrate learning. II.D.2. (Include/Grow): Learners demonstrate empathy and equity in knowledge building within the global learning community by demonstrating interest in other perspectives during learning activities. III.B.1. (Collaborate/Create): Learners participate in personal, social, and intellectual networks by using a variety of communication tools and resources. V.A.1. (Explore/Think): Learners develop and satisfy personal curiosity by reading widely and deeply in multiple formats and write and create for a variety of purposes.	Art: Anchor Standard 6. Convey meaning through the presentation of artistic work. Anchor Standard 10. Synthesize and relate knowledge and personal experiences to make art. ELA: 4. Students adjust their use of spoken, written, and visual language (e.g., conventions, style, vocabulary) to communicate effectively with a variety of audiences and for different purposes. ELA: 8. Students use a variety of technological and information resources (e.g., libraries, databases, computer networks, video) to gather and synthesize information and to create and communicate knowledge. Technology: Creative Communicator 6b. Students create original works or responsibly repurpose or remix digital resources into new creations. Creative Communicator 6d. Students publish or present content that customizes the message and medium for their intended audiences.

(cont'd)

TABLE I.1

Learning Centers and Standards (cont'd)

Learning Center	AASL Standards Framework for Learners	Content-Area Standards

Video Book Review*
 	
Learners write and film short book reviews.
 	
Page 79
	I.A.2. (Inquire/Think): Learners display curiosity and initiative by recalling prior and background knowledge as context for new meaning.
	
	I.B.3. (Inquire/Create): Learners engage with new knowledge by following a process that includes generating products that illustrate learning.
	
	I.C. (Inquire/Share): Learners adapt, communicate, and exchange learning products with others in a cycle that includes:
	  1. Interacting with content presented by others.
	  4. Sharing products with an authentic audience.
	
	III.B.1. (Collaborate/Create): Learners participate in personal, social, and intellectual networks by using a variety of communication tools and resources.
	
	IV.A.3. (Curate/Think): Learners act on an information need by making critical choices about information sources to use.
	
	V.A.1. (Explore/Think): Learners develop and satisfy personal curiosity by reading widely and deeply in multiple formats and write and create for a variety of purposes.
	
	VI.D.1. (Engage/Grow): Learners engage with information to extend personal learning by personalizing their use of information and information technologies.
		ELA: 4. Students adjust their use of spoken, written, and visual language (e.g., conventions, style, vocabulary) to communicate effectively with a variety of audiences and for different purposes.
		
		ELA: 6. Students apply knowledge of language structure, language conventions (e.g., spelling and punctuation), media techniques, figurative language, and genre to create, critique, and discuss print and non-print texts.
		
		ELA: 8. Students use a variety of technological and information resources (e.g., libraries, databases, computer networks, video) to gather and synthesize information and to create and communicate knowledge.
		
		Technology: Creative Communicator 6b. Students create original works or responsibly repurpose or remix digital resources into new creations.
		
		Creative Communicator 6d. Students publish or present content that customizes the message and medium for their intended audiences.

Learning Center	AASL Standards Framework for Learners	Content-Area Standards
Book Trailer Learners create video book trailers using iMovie or similar apps. Page 84	I.B.3. (Inquire/Create): Learners engage with new knowledge by following a process that includes generating products that illustrate learning. I.C.4. (Inquire/Share): Learners adapt, communicate, and exchange learning products with others in a cycle that includes sharing products with an authentic audience. IV.C.2. (Curate/Share): Learners exchange information resources within and beyond their learning community by contributing to collaboratively constructed information sites by ethically using and reproducing others' work. V.A.1. (Explore/Think): Learners develop and satisfy personal curiosity by reading widely and deeply in multiple formats and write and create for a variety of purposes. VI.C. (Engage/Share): Learners responsibly, ethically, and legally share new information with a global community by: 1. Sharing information resources in accordance with modification, reuse, and remix policies. 2. Disseminating new knowledge through means appropriate for the intended audience. VI.D.1. (Engage/Grow): Learners engage with information to extend personal learning by personalizing their use of information and information technologies.	ELA: 6. Students apply knowledge of language structure, language conventions (e.g., spelling and punctuation), media techniques, figurative language, and genre to create, critique, and discuss print and non-print texts. ELA: 8. Students use a variety of technological and information resources (e.g., libraries, databases, computer networks, video) to gather and synthesize information and to create and communicate knowledge. ELA: 12. Students use spoken, written, and visual language to accomplish their own purposes (e.g., for learning, enjoyment, persuasion, and the exchange of information). Technology: Digital Citizen 2c. Demonstrate an understanding of and respect for the rights and obligations of using and sharing intellectual property. Creative Communicator 6b. Students create original works or responsibly repurpose or remix digital resources into new creations. Creative Communicator 6d. Students publish or present content that customizes the message and medium for their intended audiences.

(cont'd)

Learning Centers and Standards (cont'd)

Learning Center	AASL Standards Framework for Learners	Content-Area Standards
LEGO Story Learners create story scenes using LEGOs and then film and narrate the story. Page 90	I.B.3. (Inquire/Create): Learners engage with new knowledge by following a process that includes generating products that illustrate learning. 1.C.4. (Inquire/Share): Learners adapt, communicate, and exchange learning products with others in a cycle that includes sharing products with an authentic audience. V.A.1. (Explore/Think): Learners develop and satisfy personal curiosity by reading widely and deeply in multiple formats and write and create for a variety of purposes. V.B.2. (Explore/Create): Learners construct new knowledge by persisting through self-directed pursuits by tinkering and making.	Art: Anchor Standard 1. Generate and conceptualize artistic ideas and work. Anchor Standard 6. Convey meaning through the presentation of artistic work. ELA: 4. Students adjust their use of spoken, written, and visual language (e.g., conventions, style, vocabulary) to communicate effectively with a variety of audiences and for different purposes. ELA: 6. Students apply knowledge of language structure, language conventions (e.g., spelling and punctuation), media techniques, figurative language, and genre to create, critique, and discuss print and non-print texts. Technology: Innovative Designer 4d. Students exhibit a tolerance for ambiguity, perseverance and the capacity to work with open-ended problems. Creative Communicator 6b. Students create original works or responsibly repurpose or remix digital resources into new creations.
Mini-Anagram* Learners use the letters in a given word to create as many new words as possible. Page 96	I.A.2. (Inquire/Think): Learners display curiosity and initiative by recalling prior and background knowledge as context for new meaning. V.A.1. (Explore/Think): Learners develop and satisfy personal curiosity by reading widely and deeply in multiple formats and write and create for a variety of purposes.	ELA: 6. Students apply knowledge of language structure, language conventions (e.g., spelling and punctuation), media techniques, figurative language, and genre to create, critique, and discuss print and non-print texts.

Learning Center	AASL Standards Framework for Learners	Content-Area Standards
Blackout Poetry* Learners use pages from discarded books and magazines to create poems by blacking out unwanted words with markers. Page 102	I.B.3. (Inquire/Create): Learners engage with new knowledge by following a process that includes generating products that illustrate learning. V.A.1. (Explore/Think): Learners develop and satisfy personal curiosity by reading widely and deeply in multiple formats and write and create for a variety of purposes.	Art: Anchor Standard 1. Generate and conceptualize artistic ideas and work. ELA: 3. Students apply a wide range of strategies to comprehend, interpret, evaluate, and appreciate texts. They draw on their prior experience, their interactions with other readers and writers, their knowledge of word meaning and of other texts, their word identification strategies, and their understanding of textual features (e.g., sound-letter correspondence, sentence structure, context, graphics). ELA: 5. Students employ a wide range of strategies as they write and use different writing process elements appropriately to communicate with different audiences for a variety of purposes. ELA 6. Students apply knowledge of language structure, language conventions (e.g., spelling and punctuation), media techniques, figurative language, and genre to create, critique, and discuss print and non-print texts.
Word Drawing* Learners create concrete poems by cutting and pasting words from discarded books and magazines into templates. Page 106	I.B.3. (Inquire/Create): Learners engage with new knowledge by following a process that includes generating products that illustrate learning. V.A.1. (Explore/Think): Learners develop and satisfy personal curiosity by reading widely and deeply in multiple formats and write and create for a variety of purposes.	Art: Anchor Standard 1. Generate and conceptualize artistic ideas and work. ELA: 4. Students adjust their use of spoken, written, and visual language (e.g., conventions, style, vocabulary) to communicate effectively with a variety of audiences and for different purposes. ELA: 5. Students employ a wide range of strategies as they write and use different writing process elements appropriately to communicate with different audiences for a variety of purposes. ELA 6. Students apply knowledge of language structure, language conventions (e.g., spelling and punctuation), media techniques, figurative language, and genre to create, critique, and discuss print and non-print texts.

(cont'd)

TABLE I.1

Learning Centers and Standards (cont'd)

Learning Center	AASL Standards Framework for Learners	Content-Area Standards
Photo-Book Learners read information about an animal in a photicular book, such as *Dinosaur* by Dan Kainen and Kathy Wollard, and answer questions on the sheet provided. Page 119	I.B.1. (Inquire/Create): Learners engage with new knowledge by following a process that includes using evidence to investigate questions. IV.B.4. (Curate/Create): Learners gather information appropriate to the task by organizing information by priority, topic, or other systematic scheme. V.A. (Explore/Think): Learners develop and satisfy personal curiosity by: 1. Reading widely and deeply in multiple formats and write and create for a variety of purposes. 3. Engaging in inquiry-based processes for personal growth.	ELA: 3. Students apply a wide range of strategies to comprehend, interpret, evaluate, and appreciate texts. They draw on their prior experience, their interactions with other readers and writers, their knowledge of word meaning and of other texts, their word identification strategies, and their understanding of textual features (e.g., sound-letter correspondence, sentence structure, context, graphics). ELA: 5. Students employ a wide range of strategies as they write and use different writing process elements appropriately to communicate with different audiences for a variety of purposes. Science: Obtain information using various texts, text features (e.g., headings, tables of contents, glossaries, electronic menus, icons), and other media that will be useful in answering a scientific question. (2-ESS2-3) Read grade-appropriate texts and/or use media to obtain scientific information to describe patterns in the natural world. (K-ESS3-2)
Book Spine Poetry* Learners take books from the stacks and line up the spines in order to create poems when the titles are read top to bottom. Page 122	I.B.3. (Inquire/Create): Learners engage with new knowledge by following a process that includes generating products that illustrate learning. IV.B.1. (Curate/Create): Learners gather information appropriate to the task by seeking a variety of sources. V.A.1. (Explore/Think): Learners develop and satisfy personal curiosity by reading widely and deeply in multiple formats and write and create for a variety of purposes.	ELA: 4. Students adjust their use of spoken, written, and visual language (e.g., conventions, style, vocabulary) to communicate effectively with a variety of audiences and for different purposes. ELA: 5. Students employ a wide range of strategies as they write and use different writing process elements appropriately to communicate with different audiences for a variety of purposes. ELA: 6. Students apply knowledge of language structure, language conventions (e.g., spelling and punctuation), media techniques, figurative language, and genre to create, critique, and discuss print and non-print texts.

Learning Center	AASL Standards Framework for Learners	Content-Area Standards
Grammar Hunt* Using pages from weeded books and magazines, learners cut out nouns, verbs, adjectives, or adverbs (words or pictures) and paste them on a template bearing the definition. Page 127	I.A.2. (Inquire/Think): Learners display curiosity and initiative by recalling prior and background knowledge as context for new meaning. I.B.3. (Inquire/Create): Learners engage with new knowledge by following a process that includes generating products that illustrate learning.	Art: Anchor Standard 1. Generate and conceptualize artistic ideas and work. Anchor Standard 6. Convey meaning through the presentation of artistic work. ELA: 3. Students apply a wide range of strategies to comprehend, interpret, evaluate, and appreciate texts. They draw on their prior experience, their interactions with other readers and writers, their knowledge of word meaning and of other texts, their word identification strategies, and their understanding of textual features (e.g., sound-letter correspondence, sentence structure, context, graphics).
Endangered Books Learners choose books to "save" from extinction. They choose picture books from the Endangered Book Cart to read and evaluate before making a recommendation. Page 138	I.D.4. (Inquire/Grow): Learners participate in an ongoing inquiry-based process by using reflection to guide informed decisions. IV.B.3. (Curate/Create): Learners gather information appropriate to the task by systematically questioning and assessing the validity and accuracy of information. IV.D. (Curate/Grow): Learners select and organize information for a variety of audiences by: 1. Performing ongoing analysis of and reflection on the quality, usefulness, and accuracy of curated resources. 3. Openly communicating curation processes for others to use, interpret, and validate. V.A.1. (Explore/Think): Learners develop and satisfy personal curiosity by reading widely and deeply in multiple formats and write and create for a variety of purposes.	ELA: 3. Students apply a wide range of strategies to comprehend, interpret, evaluate, and appreciate texts. They draw on their prior experience, their interactions with other readers and writers, their knowledge of word meaning and of other texts, their word identification strategies, and their understanding of textual features (e.g., sound-letter correspondence, sentence structure, context, graphics). ELA: 5. Students employ a wide range of strategies as they write and use different writing process elements appropriately to communicate with different audiences for a variety of purposes. ELA: 6. Students apply knowledge of language structure, language conventions (e.g., spelling and punctuation), media techniques, figurative language, and genre to create, critique, and discuss print and non-print texts.
Book Cart Learners put weeded books in alphabetical or decimal order on book carts. Page 142	I.A.2. (Inquire/Think): Learners display curiosity and initiative by recalling prior and background knowledge as context for new meaning.	ELA: 3. Students apply a wide range of strategies to comprehend, interpret, evaluate, and appreciate texts. They draw on their prior experience, their interactions with other readers and writers, their knowledge of word meaning and of other texts, their word identification strategies, and their understanding of textual features (e.g., sound-letter correspondence, sentence structure, context, graphics). Math: Numbers and Operations: Understand numbers, ways of representing numbers, relationships among numbers, and number systems.

(cont'd)

Learning Centers and Standards (cont'd)

Learning Center	AASL Standards Framework for Learners	Content-Area Standards
Database Exploration* Learners use tablets or laptops to explore databases, generate questions, and learn about topics of personal interest. Page 148	I.A.1. (Inquire/Think): Learners display curiosity and initiative by formulating questions about a personal interest or a curricular topic. I.B.1. (Inquire/Create): Learners engage with new knowledge by following a process that includes using evidence to investigate questions. IV.A. (Curate/Think): Learners act on an information need by: 2. Identifying possible sources of information. 3. Making critical choices about information sources to use. V.C.1. (Explore/Share): Learners engage with the learning community by expressing curiosity about a topic of personal interest or curricular relevance. VI.A. (Engage/Think): Learners follow ethical and legal guidelines for gathering and using information by: 1. Responsibly applying information, technology, and media to learning. 2. Understanding the ethical use of information, technology, and media. 3. Evaluating information for accuracy, validity, social and cultural context, and appropriateness for need. VI.B. (Engage/Create): Learners use valid information and reasoned conclusions to make ethical decisions in the creation of knowledge by: 1. Ethically using and reproducing others' work. 2. Acknowledging authorship and demonstrating respect for the intellectual property of others. 3. Including elements in personal-knowledge products that allow others to credit content appropriately.	ELA: 7. Students conduct research on issues and interests by generating ideas and questions, and by posing problems. They gather, evaluate, and synthesize data from a variety of sources (e.g., print and non-print texts, artifacts, people) to communicate their discoveries in ways that suit their purpose and audience. ELA: 8. Students use a variety of technological and information resources (e.g., libraries, databases, computer networks, video) to gather and synthesize information and to create and communicate knowledge. Technology: Constructor 3c. Students curate information from digital resources using a variety of tools and methods to create collections of artifacts that demonstrate meaningful connections or conclusions. Digital Citizen 2c. Demonstrate an understanding of and respect for the rights and obligations of using and sharing intellectual property.

Learning Center	AASL Standards Framework for Learners	Content-Area Standards

Resource Investigation*
 	
Learners use resources (atlas, almanac, encyclopedia, dictionary, thesaurus, database) to answer questions.
 	
Page 154
	IV.A. (Curate/Think): Learners act on an information need by:
	  1. Determining the need to gather information.
	  2. Identifying possible sources of information.
	  3. Making critical choices about information sources to use.
	
	V.A. (Explore/Think): Learners develop and satisfy personal curiosity by:
	  1. Reading widely and deeply in multiple formats and write and create for a variety of purposes.
	  3. Engaging in inquiry-based processes for personal growth.
		ELA: 8. Students use a variety of technological and information resources (e.g., libraries, databases, computer networks, video) to gather and synthesize information and to create and communicate knowledge.

Geography* Learners complete map puzzles and then answer geography questions using atlases. Page 162	I.B.1. (Inquire/Create): Learners engage with new knowledge by following a process that includes using evidence to investigate questions. IV.A.2. (Curate/Think): Learners act on an information need by identifying possible sources of information.	ELA: 8. Students use a variety of technological and information resources (e.g., libraries, databases, computer networks, video) to gather and synthesize information and to create and communicate knowledge. Social Studies: D2.Geo.1.3-5. Construct maps and other graphic representations of both familiar and unfamiliar places. D2.Geo.2.3-5. Use maps, satellite images, photographs, and other representations to explain relationships between the locations of places and regions and their environmental characteristics.
Abstract Collage* Learners make collages based on abstract themes by cutting pictures and words from discarded books and magazines. Page 172	I.B.3. (Inquire/Create): Learners engage with new knowledge by following a process that includes generating products that illustrate learning. V.A.1. (Explore/Think): Learners develop and satisfy personal curiosity by reading widely and deeply in multiple formats and write and create for a variety of purposes.	Art: Anchor Standard 1. Generate and conceptualize artistic ideas and work. Anchor Standard 6. Convey meaning through the presentation of artistic work. ELA: 6. Students apply knowledge of language structure, language conventions (e.g., spelling and punctuation), media techniques, figurative language, and genre to create, critique, and discuss print and non-print texts. ELA: 12. Students use spoken, written, and visual language to accomplish their own purposes (e.g., for learning, enjoyment, persuasion, and the exchange of information).

(cont'd)

TABLE I.1

Learning Centers and Standards (cont'd)

Learning Center	AASL Standards Framework for Learners	Content-Area Standards

Mystery Box*
 	
Learners are given a box containing random objects. They collaborate to find similarities, such as color, shape, or use, between pairs of objects.
 	
Page 183
	I.A.2. (Inquire/Think): Learners display curiosity and initiative by recalling prior and background knowledge as context for new meaning.
	
	II.B. (Include/Create): Learners adjust their awareness of the global learning community by:
	  1. Interacting with learners who reflect a range of perspectives.
	  2. Evaluating a variety of perspectives during learning activities.
	  3. Representing diverse perspectives during learning activities.
		ELA: 4. Students adjust their use of spoken, written, and visual language (e.g., conventions, style, vocabulary) to communicate effectively with a variety of audiences and for different purposes.
		
		ELA: 11. Students participate as knowledgeable, reflective, creative, and critical members of a variety of literacy communities.
		
		ELA: 12. Students use spoken, written, and visual language to accomplish their own purposes (e.g., for learning, enjoyment, persuasion, and the exchange of information).

Breakout Box*
 	
Learners collaborate to complete different challenges to learn the combination of one or more locks and then open toolboxes.
 	
Page 189
	I.A.2. (Inquire/Think): Learners display curiosity and initiative by recalling prior and background knowledge as context for new meaning.
	
	II.C. (Include/Share): Learners exhibit empathy with and tolerance for diverse ideas by:
	  1. Engaging in informed conversation and active debate.
	  2. Contributing to discussions in which multiple viewpoints on a topic are expressed.
	
	III.A.2. (Collaborate/Think): Learners identify collaborative opportunities by developing new understandings through engagement in a learning group.
	
	III.D. (Collaborate/Grow): Learners actively participate with others in learning situations by:
	  1. Actively contributing to group discussions.
	  2. Recognizing learning as a social responsibility.
		ELA: 3. Students apply a wide range of strategies to comprehend, interpret, evaluate, and appreciate texts. They draw on their prior experience, their interactions with other readers and writers, their knowledge of word meaning and of other texts, their word identification strategies, and their understanding of textual features (e.g., sound-letter correspondence, sentence structure, context, graphics).
		
		ELA: 11. Students participate as knowledgeable, reflective, creative, and critical members of a variety of literacy communities.
		
		Math: Numbers and Operations: Understand numbers, ways of representing numbers, relationships among numbers, and number systems
		
		Problem Solving: Solve problems that arise in mathematics and in other contexts.
		
		Science: Obtain information using various texts, text features (e.g., headings, tables of contents, glossaries, electronic menus, icons), and other media that will be useful in answering a scientific question. (2-ESS2-3)
		
		Social Studies: D2.His.10.3-5. Compare information provided by different historical sources about the past.

Learning Center	AASL Standards Framework for Learners	Content-Area Standards
Book Sort Geometry Learners collaborate to sort books into different categories. Next, they measure each book and use the data in math problems. Page 216	II.A.1. (Include/Think): Learners contribute a balanced perspective when participating in a learning community by articulating an awareness of the contributions of a range of learners. V.C. (Explore/Share): Learners engage with the learning community by: 2. Co-constructing innovative means of investigation. 3. Collaboratively identifying innovative solutions to a challenge or problem.	ELA: 6. Students apply knowledge of language structure, language conventions (e.g., spelling and punctuation), media techniques, figurative language, and genre to create, critique, and discuss print and non-print texts. ELA: 11. Students participate as knowledgeable, reflective, creative, and critical members of a variety of literacy communities. Math: Measurement: Apply appropriate techniques, tools, and formulas to determine measurements. Geometry: Analyze characteristics and properties of two- and three-dimensional geometric shapes and develop mathematical arguments about geometric relationships. Number and Operations: Compute fluently and make reasonable estimates. Problem Solving: Solve problems that arise in mathematics and in other contexts.

Part I

CHAPTER 1

Learning Centers

B efore getting into the nuts and bolts of learning centers, it's probably a good idea to start with a clear definition. This is especially true if learning centers are a new concept for you. However, even if you've already used learning centers in your school library, this chapter is helpful. It defines learning centers as they relate to this book and includes research to support using them.

THE DEFINITION

Centers or stations aren't a new concept in education. Many classroom educators already use these structures, often to teach math and literacy. Learning centers are focused, self-directed activities set up in different areas of the classroom or school library where learners work independently or collaboratively. In some classes the learner chooses which center to visit, but in others the educator assigns these. Centers are an interesting way to differentiate instruction and target multiple skills while the educator works with small groups.

Learning centers work equally well in the school library where makerspaces have paved the way for innovative library instruction. Makerspaces can vary drastically according to setting, participant grade level, budget, and purpose. In general they're places where learners have choice and where learners make something. Many learning centers, especially the maker centers, share these qualities.

Each learning center offers a different activity or challenge. Learners choose a center, complete the task, share their work, and clean up. Depending on the time available, learners may be able to visit more than one center. Learning centers are flexible and easily adapted to different schedules, grade levels, and content.

THE BENEFITS

Learning centers have numerous benefits for both school librarians and learners. They can help school librarians juggle the instructional and administrative parts of the role. When learners are working independently, the school librarian is better able to work with individuals, conduct readers' advisory, and facilitate book check-out. It can be difficult to support learners during book selection and checkout while supervising others and providing a meaningful lesson. This is especially true if you have no assistant and limited time.

Although there are distinct advantages for school librarians who offer learning centers, including opportunities to collaborate with content-area educators, learners are the main beneficiaries. Learning centers offer differentiated instruction, encourage independence and collaboration, and build competencies and resiliency in learners. They're also fun.

Differentiation

Choice is one of the most important features of learning centers. It empowers learners to take an active role in their education and increases their buy-in. Learners are more likely to work hard at a task they've selected. Responsive Classroom—a learner-centered, social-emotional approach to teaching and discipline—stresses the power of academic choice in both the classroom and special-area subjects, like the school library. Offering choices encourages learners to "develop intrinsic motivation to learn" and "take greater responsibility for their own learning" (Center for Responsive Schools 2016, 121). Isn't this what all educators hope for? Thoughtful, independent learners will be able to use these skills throughout their lives.

For some learners, too many options can be overwhelming rather than empowering. Consider your audience when selecting which centers to offer. Younger learners or those with special needs may appreciate more limited options.

Resiliency

One of the most important attributes for academic success is resiliency. No matter how intelligent a person is, they will eventually face challenges and setbacks. How a person deals with these obstacles is what matters. Some learners, often more advanced ones, can become so used to everything being easy that they're reluctant to persevere. If something doesn't work out as planned or if they struggle with a new task, they give up. The school library presents the perfect environment for learning that it's okay to make mistakes. Everybody fails sometimes. Often, that's how progress happens. We may learn more from our mistakes than our successes.

In her book *Mindset: The New Psychology of Success* (2016), Carol Dweck writes about the importance of having a growth mindset—the belief that change is possible. Learners might not be able to complete a specific activity yet. That "yet" is hugely significant and hopeful. It suggests the promise of mastering that skill sometime in the future. Learners who embrace a growth mindset are generally more positive and willing to tackle challenges.

The AASL Standards also stress the importance of resiliency and a growth mindset. The Key Commitment of the Explore Shared Foundation is that learners will "discover and innovate in a growth mindset developed through experience and reflection" (AASL 2018, 38). Having a growth mindset makes it easier to be resilient.

Although a growth mindset, reflection, and resiliency feature prominently in the AASL Standards, not many other sets of national standards directly address these essential attributes for learning. Perhaps this omission is because resiliency is more a disposition than a skill. It's a bit trickier to teach than long division.

However, learning centers provide the opportunity to practice resiliency. For example, if you're building a bridge and it falls or doesn't work out exactly as planned, you need to start over. Becoming frustrated is part of the learning process. Being able to work past that frustration and start again is something learners will need to master. Learning centers provide a fun context in which to do so, making it even more possible for learners to persevere through setbacks toward genuine resiliency.

Most centers are set up for learners to work both independently or collaboratively, and educators may choose when or whether to intervene to facilitate learning. Instead of providing the answer, educators lead learners to consider other possibilities by asking key questions. To an adult, it may be obvious that no matter how much glue stick learners use, those heavy pieces of cardboard won't stay together. But educators shouldn't steal learners' struggle. The finished product is not as important as how learners get there. Learners are working toward becoming self-sufficient. Experiencing small obstacles and failures in a safe environment prepares them to handle bigger obstacles on their own later.

Play

Fun in education is often underrated. When we enjoy an activity, it becomes play rather than work. We tend to stay engaged longer, focus more attentively, and retain what we've learned. Unfortunately, after kindergarten most learners don't have the opportunity to play in school outside recess. Modern education focuses heavily on testing and covering standards according to a timeline, both of which can cause stress and neither of which is very fun!

A visitor to your school library may question why learners are working with LEGOs. They may see this as "just playing," with an implicit message that play doesn't belong in school. Learning is a serious business. *Play*, however, is not a dirty word, nor should we be embarrassed to use it in connection to learning centers. This isn't an either-or situation. Something can be fun *and* educational. Numerous psychologists and educational researchers—including Jung, Piaget, and Erikson—have studied the role of play, demonstrating its effectiveness and importance in child development and education.

First, play helps facilitate brain development, and not just in early childhood. The book *Einstein Never Used Flash Cards: How Our Children Really Learn—And Why They Need to Play More and Memorize Less* provides evidence-based explanations about the role of play in brain development and learning. "Play promotes problem solving and creativity. It also helps to build better attention spans and encourages social development" (Hirsh-Pasek, Golinkoff, and Eyer 2004, 206). Play also can lead to higher reading levels and IQ, as well as greater imagination and innovation in learners. The truly creative inventors and innovators in society must "go beyond finding answers to already formulated problems" (215). Through play, learners are able to practice these skills.

Second, play relieves stress. Learners today are often overscheduled both in and out of school. Many are engaged in so many extracurricular activities that they have little free time for fun, relaxation, and creativity. School days can often seem like a triathlon, rushing from one activity to the next, trying to cram it all in. Who wouldn't be stressed? Erikson believed that play "is the most natural self-healing measure that childhood affords" (Erikson and Coles 2001, 113). In today's uncertain world, all learners could use more play in their lives.

The school library is the perfect place for learners to experiment without the fear of failure, where they can simply play. Learning centers also enable an autonomy and independence that learners don't often have in school, where so much of their time is directed by adults. Learning centers are fun. When learners come to the school library and see centers set up, you may hear, "Yes! It's centers." Such pure joy!

THE APPLICATION

It's my hope that you're now convinced and are excited to use learning centers. You may wonder, though, "What about everything else? What about booktalks, read-alouds, research, and all the rest?" Learning centers are meant to complement rather than replace other types of school library experiences. Learners still need direct instruction in research and library skills.

Learners love centers and get so excited to see them set up when they come to the school library. However, if centers were all learners did, some of that thrill would probably be lost. It's best to alternate learning centers with other projects or lessons. You could offer four weeks of centers and then teach learners how to use databases. You could have all grades working on centers on the same days or have just a few grades working on centers with others working on projects. You could teach research skills and then have learners cycle through the Library and Research Skills centers to practice and reinforce what they've learned. Learning centers are also great for those weeks when learners are particularly antsy, such as before and after winter break and at the end of the school year.

REFERENCES

American Association of School Librarians. 2018. *National School Library Standards for Learners, School Librarians, and School Libraries.* Chicago: ALA Editions, an Imprint of the American Library Association.

Center for Responsive Schools. 2016. *Responsive Classroom for Music, Art, PE, and Other Special Areas.* 2nd ed. Turners Falls, MA: Author.

Dweck, Carol S. 2016. *Mindset: The New Psychology of Success.* Updated ed. New York: Ballantine Books.

Erikson, Erik H., and Robert Coles. 2001. *The Erik Erikson Reader.* New York: W. W. Norton.

Hirsh-Pasek, Kathy, Roberta M. Golinkoff, and Diane E. Eyer. 2004. *Einstein Never Used Flash Cards: How Our Children Really Learn—And Why They Need to Play More and Memorize Less.* Pbk. ed. Emmaus, PA: Rodale.

CHAPTER 2

Logistics

I won't lie. A good amount of preparation goes into establishing learning centers in a school library. You have to purchase or gather the materials, make the copies, and package them all together in a storage container, but that's a one-time chore. Once you've done the initial work, most of the centers require little upkeep.

Next, you need to establish the rules and routines and then introduce each center by modeling or explaining it. Limit the number of new centers introduced at the same time, especially the more complicated ones for which learners will need adult support. Once learners are familiar with the routines and the options, learning centers tend to run themselves pretty smoothly.

When thinking of the number of centers to offer, consider how many learners can work at each center and the number of learners in the class. You want to ensure that even the last learner to pick has a few centers to choose from. Depending on class size, ten or more centers is usually enough. In the beginning consider offering more than one section of each center if you don't have enough variety.

SPACE

Learning centers can be adapted for use in any school library. Consider your library's physical layout when setting them up. Most school libraries include areas for group work with tables and chairs and perhaps an area with computers, interspersed by bookshelves. Elementary school libraries often include a story area with tiered seating. Think about how your library's layout can best be used to maximize learning and enjoyment while minimizing disruptions and conflict.

Most of the learning centers work best at tables. Limit one center per table to avoid confusion. It's best to be able to see all learners, so avoid setting up centers in the stacks if possible. Depending on how your school library is arranged, you might have to get creative. Some centers, such as Matchbox Car Engineering, Construction, and Maker Challenge, benefit from more space, so these might be set up away from the seating area, perhaps on the floor. Centers that ask learners to film a video require access to a quiet place. Consider allowing learners to use the library office, news studio, or other rooms within the main school library space.

Storage will vary according to space available. Stacking boxes on shelves in a storage room or the library office keeps them out of the way and protected. Using open shelving within the main school library space makes boxes more accessible to learners.

Another storage issue is where to keep the materials when you have back-to-back classes. This often happens in elementary schools where librarians may teach several different grade levels in a row. If the next group will be using the same centers, then materials can remain on the tables. For example, you might have a second-grade class using centers, followed by a fourth-grade class working on a research project, followed by a third-grade class using centers. It doesn't make sense to have learners put the materials away completely. It also wastes time. In this case, store the materials on top of nearby bookcases.

A final space concern may be what to do if other students are checking out books or using the school library when learning centers are going on. Many school libraries may have multiple groups using the library space at the same time. If this is the case in your school library, it will affect where you set up the centers. Be sure that learners don't block access to the bookshelves.

TIME

Time will not always be on your side. This is the reality for many school librarians and is something they often have no control over. Access to the school library varies greatly depending on grade level, school, and district. When, which, and for how long classes visit the school library are often determined by a classroom educator's need for planning time.

This is most often the case in elementary schools where the school librarian might be part of the Specials team along with art, music, and physical education. Schedules can vary widely from school to school. One school librarian might see every class for thirty minutes, including book checkout, each week, leaving little time for instruction. Other schools might have classes visit the library for forty-five minutes or an hour every other week. Some school librarians operate on a fixed schedule for book checkout but a flexible schedule for instruction. This approach enables collaboration with classroom educators and allows the school librarian to provide timely support and instruction.

To save time, you can set up centers before the class arrives. Learners can easily lose track of time, so using a visible countdown timer and giving verbal reminders ("fifteen minutes left," "five minutes until cleanup," "one minute left") would be helpful. Also, be sure to leave enough time at the end for cleanup (five to eight minutes depending on the center).

Some centers have a reflection component. It's important to leave enough time at the end for this part. It might be easier for learners to clean up first, so they won't be tempted to continue with the activity. On the other hand, it might be easier for them to reflect if the project is still in one piece. Decide what works best for your learners.

Learning centers are flexible and easily adapted for use with different scenarios. Each center description includes a suggested amount of time. Longer activities can often be broken up into different sessions. Table 2.1 offers tips for different situations.

TABLE 2.1

TIME TIPS

Time	Elementary School	Middle/High School
30 minutes	Have learners check out books first. After they check out, they can choose a center or read their books.	Middle and high school library lessons are usually a collaboration between the school librarian and the content-area educator. If you are using one of the learning center activities with a whole class, the time will vary and most likely not include book checkout.
45–60 minutes	Learners work at centers first and then clean up before checking out books. Depending on class size, twenty minutes for book selection and checkout is usually sufficient.	
Lunch	Set up a few centers for learners to use during their lunchtime or other free periods. Another option is to let learners choose from all the centers and only take those out.	
Before/ After school	This scenario is probably more likely at the middle and high school levels where learners have greater autonomy. You might set up one or two popular centers and let learners select others according to preference.	

Materials

The centers described in this book were created with thrift in mind. Whenever possible, recycled materials and weeded books and magazines are used. This approach is ecofriendly, keeps costs down, and can make it easier for school librarians who find it hard to part with books. Using discarded books in centers gives them new life and purpose.

Unfortunately, not all the materials are free. The good news is that once purchased, most materials can be used for years to come. Each center description gives tips about which materials are essential and which are optional. Table 2.2 outlines suggested shopping lists for a range of budgets.

Not all items need to come from your school library budget. Other sources of materials or funds include PTA grants, community material donations (Facebook is great for this), yard sales, DonorsChoose.org, and other organizations that offer grants to school librarians and other educators.

TABLE 2.2

MATERIAL LISTS FOR VARIOUS BUDGETS

Basic	Mid-range	Splurge
• LEGOs (bricks, people, props, plates) • Scissors • Single-hole punch • Pencils • Crayons, colored pencils, and markers (including several black ones) • Glue • Tape • Stapler and staples • Recyclables • String, yarn, and other basic art supplies • Popsicle sticks • Aluminum foil • Discarded books and magazines • Copier paper • Colored paper • Rubber bands • Rulers • Calculator • Folders • Plastic baggies • Print resources (almanac, atlas, dictionary, encyclopedias, thesaurus) • Poetry books • Shelf markers or sticky notes • Book cart or shelf and bookends • World map puzzle • U.S. map puzzle • Toolbox • Locks • Hasp	• Basic items • Tablet or laptop • Camera or video camera • iMovie app • Do Ink app • Pizza box • Green gloves • KEVA Planks • Marbles (2–10) • K'Nex • Magnetic tiles • Matching bins with lids • Hot glue gun and refill glue sticks • Yardstick or tape measure • Matchbox cars, tracks, and connectors • Goldilocks doll • Headphones • Timer • Clipboards • Photicular books: Safari; Outback; Dinosaur; Polar; Ocean; Jungle; and Wild by Dan Kainen • Origami paper • Magnetic alphabet letters • Magnetic words • Metallic cookie sheet or magnetic board	• Basic and mid-range items • Multiple tablets and laptops • KEVA Giant Foam Planks • 3-D pens and refill sticks • Zoomy digital microscope • Magnifying glass • Board games

Storing Materials

One area of choice is storage containers. Depending on your budget and need for uniformity, you have several options. If you like everything to look neat and to match, you will probably want to purchase the same style of containers with lids. The Container Store sells one type of stackable containers called Really Useful Boxes that come in various sizes and colors with lids that lock. These containers are ideal for stacking and are easy to carry. You could also use any bins you have available or even cardboard boxes. Regardless of which type of container you choose, clearly label each center. See appendix B for reproducible learning center labels.

Cleaning Materials

Before the recent pandemic, cleaning the materials at the end of the school year was enough. Of course, if someone put a LEGO in their mouth or up their nose, that item was put aside and cleaned thoroughly. Likewise, anything that someone had coughed, sneezed, or snotted on was segregated for disinfection.

Unfortunately, that level of cleaning is no longer enough. Even when sharing materials is possible again, the lessons learned through quarantine will remain. Different viruses can remain infectious for several hours to several days depending on the type of surface they land on. Most seem to live longer on hard surfaces like plastic than on paper or cardboard.

Cleaning every LEGO, block, or pencil after each learner uses it isn't practical. In this situation, time might be the easiest solution. If possible, have multiple sets of center materials that can be used and then left in quarantine for a few days before going back into rotation. Keep a bin clearly labeled "To Clean" for materials that learners have put in their mouth or sneezed on and that need more immediate cleaning.

RULES AND ROUTINES

All school librarians will set rules and routines specific to their particular situation and preferences. Although these may vary, it's important to establish rules and routines at the beginning to help learning centers run smoothly. Displaying a chart with the rules and routines and providing verbal reminders periodically are helpful. A review may be necessary when new learners arrive or when there's been a lapse between uses of a center.

Here are some rules and routines that have worked well in my elementary school library:

- Begin with all learners sitting or standing in one place (story area, big spot on the carpet, or lined up).
- List all the centers learners can choose from that day and explain how many spots are available at each. Decide beforehand how many learners can work at each center at a time. Two to four is usually appropriate. You want to ensure that enough materials are available for each learner to participate fully.
- Explain any new centers and briefly re-explain more complicated centers. If some centers require adult supervision (for example, 3-D Pens or Mini Green Screen), mention this.

- Select learners one at a time to choose centers. This could be done randomly, according to who has been listening most attentively, or according to a predetermined rotation.
- Learners may take their time choosing, but once they sit down they cannot switch to a different center for at least ten minutes. This limitation helps prevent chaos.
- Learners must work at their center for at least ten minutes before requesting to switch. To do so, they must stay at the center, raise their hand, and ask to switch. They must clean up that center before switching to another center, unless they are working with a partner. In that case, learners should ask their partner if they want help cleaning up or if the partner will clean up all materials at the end.
- Once a center is full, it's full.
- Learning centers are not spectator sports. Everyone has to choose a center and participate.
- Reading is always an option. Some learners will choose to read books or magazines instead of choosing a learning center.
- If learners are not behaving safely and respectfully (with materials or partners), they will be asked to leave the center.
- All centers must be cleaned up before learners leave. The last class of the day can put the centers away.

ASSESSMENT

In the age of high-stakes testing, the school library may be the one place where learners aren't graded. So much of education is driven by assessment that learners may be less interested in gaining knowledge or mastering skills as long as they get the grade they want. It can be hard to enjoy an activity or experience if you know you will be graded on it.

Remaining assessment-free helps the school library foster a warm, welcoming, nonjudgmental environment. Learners are able to explore and make mistakes without fear of failure. They can engage in learning for its own sake. Grades are not the only form of motivation. If presented with interesting activities and choice, the majority of learners will still try hard.

If you, your school, or district requires some form of assessment, consider using self- or peer-assessment, or both, possibly in rubric form. These types of assessments help empower learners and build new skills. Tailor your rubric or other assessment to fit with your school's grading system.

Refer to chapter 12, "Measuring Learner Growth," in the *National School Library Standards for Learners, School Librarians, and School Libraries* (AASL 2018) for a detailed discussion of assessment in the school library. That chapter includes examples and suggestions for assessment. It focuses on ways in which learners can demonstrate competencies rather than outcomes.

SHARING AND PRESERVATION OF WORK

It's important to consider how learners can share and save their work. Many of the learning centers ask learners to dismantle their creations at the end. This can be heart-breaking for some. Taking photos of the creations can help tremendously. You could periodically print these photos to share with learners or to display in the school library. You could also include the photos in a newsletter or on the school library website.

Videos provide another means of sharing and preserving learners' work. How and where will you save and share these videos? You could broadcast them on the school news show, post them on the school library website, use them as samples in a learning center, or just show them to the class. Downloading videos and printing pictures is time-consuming. Most learners will forget, so if you don't have the time or energy to download every video and picture, it's okay. Be sure to ask each learner for permission before posting or displaying any work.

COLLABORATION

Most learning centers present an opportunity for collaboration among learners and between the school librarian and other educators. The ability to collaborate well is another important life skill. Educators should provide direct instruction and many chances to practice because collaboration does not come naturally to everyone.

Learners need to know how to express ideas and give constructive criticism, stand up for their own ideas, actively listen, and compromise. They may need to know what words to use during discussion. Create a chart with sentence starters so learners have the language they need.

The school librarian should model what good collaboration looks like and sounds like. Consider using the Responsive Classroom method of instruction (Center for Responsive Schools 2016). First, the educator models the behavior. Next, one or two learners demonstrate the behavior, and, finally, the whole group practices the behavior. It would be helpful to repeat these lessons at the beginning of each school year.

Troubleshooting possible problems beforehand can also improve learner collaboration. Ask the whole group to list some problems that might happen and to brainstorm possible solutions. These could be listed on a chart and displayed for easy reference.

Learning centers also provide many opportunities to collaborate with other educators. Several of the center activities can be expanded into projects that are tailored to specific grade levels and content.

TROUBLESHOOTING

Even with meticulous preparation and management systems, problems will crop up. Any time learners are asked to interact, share materials, or even share the same space there's the chance of conflict. Being proactive can help minimize issues and even act as a learning experience in itself. Watch and listen for learners who are becoming too frustrated. The trick is to intervene before they become overwhelmed. Volume can be one of the first indications of frustration. Step in to offer support, words of encouragement, or the possibility of taking a break and returning to the center later. Stepping away from a problem and returning later give learners time to process and consider other alternatives.

Collaboration can create conflict. Many learners haven't mastered how to interact and deal with the strong emotions that can accompany working with others. Consider the individuals in your school library and their possible trigger points. Which learners should not work together? Whom will you need to keep a close eye on? By giving learners the tools to deal with their emotions, you are giving them skills they can apply throughout life.

More-specific troubleshooting tips are included in the individual center sections when applicable.

REFERENCES

American Association of School Librarians. 2018. *National School Library Standards for Learners, School Librarians, and School Libraries.* Chicago: ALA Editions, an Imprint of the American Library Association.

Center for Responsive Schools. 2016. *Responsive Classroom for Music, Art, PE, and Other Special Areas.* 2nd ed. Turners Falls, MA: Author.

Part II

CHAPTER 3

Maker Centers

M akerspaces have been popping up all over—in school and public libraries, universities, and community centers. They might vary in purpose and the activities they offer, but they share an undeniable appeal. Making things, whether with crafting materials or technology, is fun and engaging for learners of all ages.

The six centers in this chapter—Maker Challenge, Innovation Station, Simple Machines, Matchbox Car Engineering, Construction, and Fairy-Tale Challenge—are like mini-makerspaces where learners engage in hands-on, often open-ended, challenges. These centers target a variety of AASL Standards and content-area standards while learners practice critical- and creative-thinking skills and resiliency. Learners work independently or collaboratively to plan, create, improve, and reflect in a cycle similar to the engineering design process.

Although many people associate artists with creativity, engineers and scientists are perhaps the most creative individuals. They invent and innovate to find creative solutions to real-life problems. The maker centers provide similar opportunities for learners to "construct new knowledge by: (1) problem solving through cycles of design, implementation, and reflection [and] (2) persisting through self-directed pursuits by tinkering and making" (AASL 2018, Learner V.B.). Perhaps these centers will encourage more learners to pursue science, technology, engineering, and mathematics (STEM) careers.

Any center in which learners build something will be popular, so the maker centers will most likely be in high demand. Some learners would happily choose the same maker center each week. They see play and fun where the adults see learning.

Learners may not realize all the skills they're developing. One way to help create awareness is through reflection. Each maker center includes a reflection sheet, although using it isn't mandatory. It does help legitimize these centers as more than "just play," but reflection is not nearly as fun as continuing to build with LEGOs. Reflection is an important, but often neglected, part of learning. It's easy to run out of time. Considering what you've learned, even for just a few minutes, reinforces and adds closure to a lesson or experience. Reflection is embedded in the Grow Domain of the AASL Standards. Consider if, when, and how to use the reflection sheets.

After working in a maker center, learners must dismantle their creations. Some learners may be reluctant to destroy their work. This happens fairly often, especially with younger learners new to sharing materials. Give learners the option of photographing their creations. It makes them feel as if the work has been preserved and their creativity has been appreciated.

MAKER CHALLENGE CENTER

"One man's trash is another man's treasure." This saying definitely applies to the Maker Challenge center in which recyclables are the main building materials. Empty cereal boxes and paper towel rolls can be transformed into a tower. Old videocassettes form the deck of a bridge with the videotape strung as cables.

This center is inexpensive, eco-friendly, and easy to set up. Learners use string or rubber bands to hold their creations together, and at the end they dismantle their structures so the materials can be reused. Provide scissors to help undo pesky knots. Discuss how this center embraces two of the three Rs (Reduce, Reuse, Recycle) because it uses recycled materials.

Learners have to build something described on a challenge card using recycled materials. They work on creative-thinking skills and resiliency. At the end, learners complete a Maker Challenge Reflection Sheet (WS 3.3) to document their process and think about what they would change.

Include a variety of cardboard boxes, paper towel rolls, plastic containers, and random recycled objects. Use a large bin or cardboard box for storage and plan to check and replenish materials every few weeks. Ask friends and families if they have anything to donate, which will give you a nice variety of objects.

After introducing this center, you can expect most learners to be relatively self-sufficient. Rotating challenge cards keeps it fresh, so this is not a "one and done" center.

Learners may decide to work with a partner. If so, encourage them to share ideas throughout the planning and building process. Collaboration increases the variety of AASL Standards that learners work on and makes the process more fun.

Because this center uses materials found in most homes, it could easily be used as a distance learning challenge with learners posting pictures of their creations.

Objective

To complete a design challenge using recycled materials, altering and improving as needed.

AASL Standards Framework for Learners

V.B.2. (Explore/Create): Learners construct new knowledge by persisting through self-directed pursuits by tinkering and making.

V.D.(Explore/Grow): Learners develop through experience and reflection by:
1. Iteratively responding to challenges.
2. Recognizing capabilities and skills that can be developed, improved, and expanded.

Content Areas
- Art
- English/Language Arts
- Science
- Technology

Lesson Duration
15–30 minutes

Materials
- Maker Challenge Learner Directions (WS 3.1)
- Maker Challenge Cards (WS 3.2)
- Maker Challenge Reflection Sheet (WS 3.3)
- A large bin or box for storage
- A variety of recycled materials (cereal and other food boxes, paper towel rolls, plastic containers) and other random objects suitable for building
- String or yarn
- Rubber bands
- Scissors
- Ruler
- Pencils
- Camera, tablet, or phone to photograph student work (optional)

Educator Preparation
1. Gather all materials.
2. Copy the Maker Challenge Learner Directions (WS 3.1) and the Maker Challenge Cards (WS 3.2) on card stock and laminate if possible.
3. Separate the Maker Challenge Cards (WS 3.2).
4. Make several copies of the Maker Challenge Reflection Sheet (WS 3.3).
5. Place all of these in a folder or large envelope.
6. Consider and include necessary modifications and extensions.

Learner Steps

Individual
1. Learners choose one of the Maker Challenge Cards (WS 3.2) and read it.
2. Next, they brainstorm ideas and use the back of the Maker Challenge Reflection Sheet (WS 3.3) to draw their plan if they want.
3. Learners build their design, making changes as needed.

4. When finished, they fill out the Maker Challenge Reflection Sheet (WS 3.3) and, if possible, share their creation.
5. If photographing the product is an option, the school librarian or a partner should do so now.
6. Finally, learners dismantle their designs and return reusable materials to the bin.

Partner

When learners work with a partner or in small groups, the steps unfold in the same order, except learners will discuss their ideas with their partner throughout the process. Although collaborating, each learner should use their own Maker Challenge Reflection Sheet (WS 3.3). This helps ensure learner accountability.

Modifications

To support English learners, learners with special education status, and younger learners, the school librarian can
- add visual examples to the Maker Challenge Cards (WS 3.2),
- limit the choice of Maker Challenge Cards (WS 3.2), or
- encourage partner work.

Distance Learning

Post the Maker Challenge Learner Directions (WS 3.1) and one challenge at a time online. List suggested recyclable materials. Include the optional Maker Challenge Reflection Sheet (WS 3.3). Encourage learners to photograph and share their creations. Photos can be posted on the school library website, Google Classroom, or similar locale with learner permission. A good book to pair this activity with is *Iggy Peck, Architect* by Andrea Beaty.

MAKER CHALLENGE LEARNER DIRECTIONS

Task: To complete a design challenge using recycled materials, altering and improving as needed.

Steps

1. Choose a Maker Challenge Card and read it.
2. Brainstorm ideas.* Looking at the available materials can help.
3. If you want to draw your plan first, use the back of the Maker Challenge Reflection Sheet.
4. If working with a partner, make sure you share and listen to ideas before, during, and after building.
5. Begin building.
6. Remember, the ruler and scissors are tools, not building materials.
7. Make changes to your design as needed.
8. When finished, fill out the Maker Challenge Reflection Sheet.
9. Carefully take your creation apart so the materials can be used again. Discard any materials that are too small or torn up to be reused. If you're not sure, ask an adult for advice.

*If working with a partner, share and listen to ideas before, during, and after building.

MAKER CHALLENGE CARDS

Challenge 1
Build the tallest freestanding tower you can, using materials from the box.
Your tower must stand on its own without being tied to furniture or being held.

Challenge 2
Build a monument or statue for a famous person or event, using materials from the
box. Be prepared to explain how your design honors the person or event.

Challenge 3
Build a bridge, using materials from the box. Your bridge must allow 4-inch boats
to pass underneath and must hold weight on its deck without collapsing. You can
use the ruler to measure but not as part of your bridge.

Challenge 4
Build a piece of furniture for a doll or small pet, using the materials in the box.
Be prepared to explain how your furniture will be used.

Challenge 5
Build a toy, game, or piece of sports equipment, using the materials in the box.
Be prepared to explain how it works.

Challenge 6
Build something that would be helpful at school or home, using the materials in the
box. Be prepared to explain its purpose.

Challenge 7
Build a mini obstacle course, using the materials in the box. Be prepared to
demonstrate how the course works.

Challenge 8
Free choice: Build something using the materials in the box. Be prepared to
explain your creation.

MAKER CHALLENGE REFLECTION SHEET

Name _____   Class _____

Which challenge did you complete?

_____

_____

_____

Describe your creation. What is it?

_____

_____

_____

Are you happy with your creation? If yes, what do you like most about it?
If no, what doesn't work?

_____

_____

_____

If you had more time and materials, how would you change your design?

_____

_____

_____

INNOVATION STATION CENTER

Who invented the light bulb? Thomas Edison may pop into your head, but he wasn't the inventor. Joseph Swan invented the first incandescent light bulb. Edison, who modified existing designs, is often wrongly credited as the inventor.

Innovation, whereby we learn from mistakes, is often much more valuable than invention. Companies want employees who can creatively solve problems and generate new ideas. The Innovation Station center enables learners to practice these skills. It also requires minimal space and preparation, a real win-win situation.

Learners are given three Innovation Station cards and may work individually or collaboratively. They must mentally disassemble the objects pictured on the cards, listing the materials each is made of on the planning sheet. Learners should spend some time brainstorming ways in which to combine these materials. The challenge is to create a new product or innovate a new design of an existing product that uses at least one material from each of two cards.

This task can be completed in more than one session if necessary. The value is not in the final product but in the steps leading up to and following its design. At the end, learners draw and label their products. Learners will explain their product's purpose in writing and, if possible, verbally to a partner.

Objective

To use creative thinking skills to invent or innovate a product and explain its purpose in writing.

AASL Standards Framework for Learners

I.A.2. (Inquire/Think): Learners display curiosity and initiative by recalling prior and background knowledge as context for new meaning.

III.C.1. (Collaborate/Share): Learners work productively with others to solve problems by soliciting and responding to feedback from others.

V.B.1. (Explore/Create): Learners construct new knowledge by problem solving through cycles of design, implementation, and reflection.

V.C.3. (Explore/Share): Learners engage with the learning community by collaboratively identifying innovative solutions to a challenge or problem.

Content Areas

- Art
- English/Language Arts
- Science
- Technology

Lesson Duration

15–30 minutes

Materials
- Innovation Station Learner Directions (WS 3.4)
- Innovation Station Cards (WS 3.5)
- Innovation Station Planning Sheet (WS 3.6)
- Innovation Station Reflection Sheet (WS 3.7)
- Pencils
- Markers or crayons (optional)
- Concrete objects from cards (optional)

Educator Preparation
1. Copy the Innovation Station Cards (WS 3.5) on card stock and laminate if possible.
2. Cut the cards to separate.
3. Make one or two copies of the Innovation Station Learner Directions (WS 3.4) on card stock and laminate. These sheets and the object cards will be reused.
4. Make several double-sided copies of the Innovation Station Planning Sheet (WS 3.6) and Reflection Sheet (WS 3.7).
5. Place all of these in a folder or large envelope.
6. Consider and include necessary modifications and extensions.

Learner Steps

Individual
1. Learners look at one card and write the name of the object on the Innovation Station Planning Sheet (WS 3.6).
2. Learners should think about what the object is made of. What would it look like if learners took the object apart?
3. Learners write down all the component parts of the object on the paper and repeat with each card.
4. Next, learners brainstorm ways to combine the different materials and sketch their ideas in the fourth box on the Planning Sheet (WS 3.6).
5. Learners draw and label the final product on the Innovation Station Reflection Sheet (WS 3.7) and, in the last box, explain in writing what their product is or does.
6. Learners share their designs with someone else, if possible.

Partner
When learners work with a partner or in small groups, the steps unfold in the same order, except learners will discuss their ideas throughout the process with their partner(s). Although collaborating, each learner should use their own planning sheet to record ideas and sketch designs. This helps ensure learner accountability.

Modifications

This center can be challenging for English learners, learners with special education status, and younger learners who may struggle with abstract thinking and language. The school librarian can offer support by

- modeling the activity with one object first,
- allowing learners to draw rather than list each material,
- encouraging partner work, or
- providing some concrete objects pictured on the object cards for learners to physically disassemble.

Distance Learning

Post the Innovation Station Learner Directions (WS 3.4) online with three to five Innovation Station Cards (WS 3.5). Include the Innovation Station Planning Sheet (WS 3.6) and the Innovation Station Reflection Sheet (WS 3.7) as well. Learners can download and print these or complete them online if using Google Docs. Encourage learners to photograph and share their creations. Photos can be posted on the school library website, Google Classroom, or a similar outlet with learner permission. A good companion text is *The Most Magnificent Thing* by Ashley Spires.

Extensions

Advanced learners, including those at the middle and high school levels, can build on their designs with the following suggestions. These activities can also be used by learners who want to work in this center during multiple sessions.

- Learners build their design or a model if possible.
- Learners give their products new brand names and create print or video advertisements for them.

INNOVATION STATION LEARNER DIRECTIONS

Task: Create or innovate (improve) a product using materials from 2–3 different objects.

Individual	Partner
1. Look at one card.	1. Look at one card.
2. On your sheet, write the name of the object.	2. On your sheet, write the name of the object.
3. Think about what the object is made of. What would it look like if you took it apart?	3. Think about what the object is made of. What would it look like if you took it apart?
4. Write down all the materials on your paper.	4. Share your ideas with your partner.
5. Repeat with each card.	5. Write down all the materials on your planning sheet.
6. Brainstorm ways to combine the different materials.	6. Repeat with each card.
7. Sketch your idea in the fourth box on the planning sheet.	7. Brainstorm ways to combine the different materials.
8. Draw and label the final product on the Innovation Station Reflection Sheet.	8. Sketch your idea in the fourth box on the planning sheet.
9. Explain what your product is or does in the last box.	9. Take turns sharing ideas with your partner. Decide if you will choose one of the ideas, combine them, or work on separate designs.
10. Share your design with someone if possible.	10. Draw and label the final product on the Innovation Station Reflection Sheet.
	11. Explain what your product is or does in the last box.

INNOVATION STATION CARDS

Bicycle

Umbrella

Sunglasses

Cowboy Hat

INNOVATION STATION CARDS (*cont'd*)

Shopping Cart

Kite

Trampoline

Stapler

Skateboard

Backpack

Guitar

Rake

INNOVATION STATION CARDS (*cont'd*)

Sandal

Tennis Racket

Tape Dispenser

Scissors

WORKSHEET 3.6

INNOVATION STATION PLANNING SHEET

Name _____   Class _____

Object: _____ Materials:	Object: _____ Materials:
Object: _____ Materials:	Draw your idea here.

INNOVATION STATION REFLECTION SHEET

Name _____   Class _____

Draw your product below. Label each part to show the materials you used.

Describe your product. What does it do?

SIMPLE MACHINES CENTER

Scissors, staplers, pencil sharpeners, ramps, bicycles—all rely on simple machines. It's amazing how many everyday objects feature simple machines.

These science concepts are often introduced in the early primary grades, with a more in-depth focus by third grade. This center could be used to teach or reinforce the different types and uses of simple machines. It also presents an opportunity to collaborate with the classroom or STEM educator.

In this center, learners build models of playground equipment that feature simple machines (pulley, screw, wheel and axle, wedge, lever, and inclined plane). Learners can relate to playgrounds, making this center more authentic. If collaborating with another educator and using this activity with a whole class, consider having learners begin by studying the playground equipment at your school. They can analyze simple machines already in use and brainstorm ideas for new equipment.

This center includes different direction sheets for each simple machine with descriptions and pictures for reference. All materials and directions can be kept together, or you can create a different materials box for each simple machine. There are advantages and disadvantages to both options. Keeping each simple machine separate provides structure for learners who need more support. Materials can be better tailored to the specific task. For more advanced learners, however, this separation decreases the challenge. You will also decide whether to set the challenge for the day or allow learners to choose for themselves. Another option is to set up several centers, each with a different simple machine.

This center works equally well as a partner or individual activity. Collaboration, though valuable and often necessary, usually takes longer and complicates matters by introducing the question of what to do with the finished product. Here are some ideas that answer this question.

1. Learners can keep their creations. For partners, this solution works only if one learner is willing to let the other learner take the object home.
2. Learners can dismantle the creation, putting aside materials that can be reused. Photographing the work can make this choice easier to accept.
3. A fun option, if space is available, is to display work from this center in the school library, creating a model playground. If learners opt to display their work, ask them to add a note card with their name, class, and a short description including the type of simple machine used.

Objective
To plan and build a model of playground equipment including a simple machine.

AASL Standards Framework for Learners

V.B. (Explore/Create): Learners construct new knowledge by:

1. Problem solving through cycles of design, implementation, and reflection.
2. Persisting through self-directed pursuits by tinkering and making.

V.C.3. (Explore/Share): Learners engage with the learning community by collaboratively identifying innovative solutions to a challenge or problem.

Content Areas

- English/Language Arts
- Science
- Technology

Lesson Duration

15–45 minutes (this center can be stretched to multiple sessions)

Materials

- Simple Machines Learner Directions (WS 3.8–WS 3.13)
- Simple Machines Planning Sheet (WS 3.14)
- Simple Machines Reflection Sheet (WS 3.15)
- Recycled materials such as cardboard boxes, paper towel rolls, and plastic containers
- Paper (construction paper, card stock, index cards, etc.)
- Popsicle sticks
- Yarn, string, rope, or ribbon
- Aluminum foil (optional)
- Scissors
- Single-hole punch
- Staplers
- Masking or other types of sturdy tape
- Liquid glue
- Hot glue gun and refill glue sticks (optional)
- Camera or tablet (optional)
- Pencils

Educator Preparation

1. Gather all materials.
2. Make sure learners have a variety of materials to choose from to make the activity challenging and creative.

3. Copy the Simple Machines Learner Directions (WS 3.8–WS 3.13) on separate sheets of card stock and laminate if possible.
4. Make several double-sided copies of the Simple Machines Planning Sheet (WS 3.14) and the Simple Machines Reflection Sheet (WS 3.15).

 TROUBLESHOOTING

Some of the simple machines require certain materials. For example, the pulley needs a sturdy box or similar object to hang from. The lever should be made from unbendable material such as a popsicle stick.

Learner Steps

Individual

1. Learners read one of the Simple Machines Learner Directions (WS 3.8–WS 3.13) including the definition.
2. Learners think about types of playground equipment that use that particular simple machine.
3. Learners draw their ideas on the Simple Machines Planning Sheet (WS 3.14) and then choose materials to build their design.
4. Learners build, test, and change their design as needed.
5. When finished, learners complete the Simple Machines Reflection Sheet (WS 3.15) and, if possible, share their design.

Partner

When working with a partner, learners should focus on sharing and listening to ideas throughout the activity. Some groups may decide to work on the same model, whereas others might build separate models and then combine them. Encourage learners to provide feedback to each other even if they're working on separate designs. Regardless, learners should be held accountable by completing individual Simple Machines Planning Sheets (WS 3.14) and Simple Machines Reflection Sheets (WS 3.15).

Modifications

To support English learners, learners with special education status, and younger learners, the school librarian can

- limit the choice of task and materials,
- encourage partner work,
- include pictures of playground equipment, or
- provide concrete examples of the simple machines for learners to explore.

Distance Learning

Post one Simple Machines Learner Directions (WS 3.8–3.13) at a time online and list suggested recyclable materials to use. Include images of playground equipment for reference. Upload the Simple Machines Planning Sheet (WS 3.14) and the Simple Machines Reflection Sheet (WS 3.15). Encourage learners to photograph and share their creations. Photos can be posted on the school library website, Google Classroom, or a similar outlet with learner permission.

Extensions

Challenge advanced learners to include multiple simple machines in the same design.

SIMPLE MACHINES LEARNER DIRECTIONS: PULLEY

Pulley. A simple machine that uses a rope or string looped over a wheel to lift heavy objects

Task: To plan and build a model of playground equipment including a pulley.

Steps

1. Read the definition and look at the picture.
2. Think about types of playground equipment that would use a pulley.
3. Draw your ideas on the Simple Machines Planning Sheet.*
4. Choose materials to build your design.
5. Build, testing and changing your design as needed.
6. Complete the Simple Machines Reflection Sheet.
7. Share your design if possible.
8. Clean up.

*If working with a partner, share and listen to ideas before, during, and after building.

SIMPLE MACHINES LEARNER DIRECTIONS: INCLINED PLANE

Inclined Plane. A simple machine that looks like a rectangle tilted uphill with triangular sides or a slice of cake lying on its side. Inclined planes use slope to make work easier and do not move.

Task: To plan and build a model of playground equipment including an inclined plane.

Steps
1. Read the definition and look at the picture.
2. Think about types of playground equipment that would use an inclined plane.
3. Draw your ideas on the Simple Machines Planning Sheet.*
4. Choose materials to build your design.
5. Build, testing and changing your design as needed.
6. Complete the Simple Machines Reflection Sheet.
7. Share your design if possible.
8. Clean up.

*If working with a partner, share and listen to ideas before, during, and after building.

SIMPLE MACHINES LEARNER DIRECTIONS: WHEEL AND AXLE

Wheel and Axle. A simple machine made up of a round wheel attached to a cylinder-shaped axle. These parts work together and rotate, sometimes with the help of a pulley or rope.

Task: To plan and build a model of playground equipment including a wheel and axle.

Steps

1. Read the definition and look at the picture.
2. Think about types of playground equipment that would use a wheel and axle.
3. Draw your ideas on the Simple Machines Planning Sheet.*
4. Choose materials to build your design.
5. Build, testing and changing your design as needed.
6. Complete the Simple Machines Reflection Sheet.
7. Share your design if possible.
8. Clean up.

*If working with a partner, share and listen to ideas before, during, and after building.

SIMPLE MACHINES LEARNER DIRECTIONS: SCREW

Screw. A simple machine shaped like a cylinder with a pointed tip and a spiral-shaped thread. A force is applied at the head to turn the screw and move it forward.

Task: To plan and build a model of playground equipment including a screw.

Steps

1. Read the definition and look at the picture.
2. Think about types of playground equipment that would use a screw.
3. Draw your ideas on the Simple Machines Planning Sheet.*
4. Choose materials to build your design.
5. Build, testing and changing your design as needed.
6. Complete the Simple Machines Reflection Sheet.
7. Share your design if possible.
8. Clean up.

*If working with a partner, share and listen to ideas before, during, and after building.

SIMPLE MACHINES LEARNER DIRECTIONS: LEVER

Lever. A simple machine that uses a bar or beam resting on a fulcrum. Pressing on one end of the lever creates a force at the other end to lift heavy objects.

Task: To plan and build a model of playground equipment including a lever.

Steps

1. Read the definition and look at the picture.
2. Think about types of playground equipment that would use a lever.
3. Draw your ideas on the Simple Machines Planning Sheet.*
4. Choose materials to build your design.
5. Build, testing and changing your design as needed.
6. Complete the Simple Machines Reflection Sheet.
7 Share your design if possible.
8. Clean up.

*If working with a partner, share and listen to ideas before, during, and after building.

SIMPLE MACHINES LEARNER DIRECTIONS: WEDGE

Wedge. A simple machine made of two triangular sides with a flat top and bottom like a slice of cake. A wedge looks like an inclined plane except it moves, usually balancing on the narrow end with force applied to the thick end.

Task: To plan and build a model of playground equipment including a wedge.

Steps

1. Read the definition and look at the picture.
2. Think about types of playground equipment that would use a wedge.
3. Draw your ideas on the Simple Machines Planning Sheet.*
4. Choose materials to build your design.
5. Build, testing and changing your design as needed.
6. Complete the Simple Machines Reflection Sheet.
7. Share your design if possible.
8. Clean up.

*If working with a partner, share and listen to ideas before, during, and after building.

SIMPLE MACHINES PLANNING SHEET

Name _____ Class _____

Simple Machine:

_____

Type of Playground Equipment:

_____

_____

_____

Draw your plan here.

WORKSHEET 3.15

SIMPLE MACHINES REFLECTION SHEET

Name   Class

What did you build, and how does it work?

Explain the steps in your process. Include any problems you might have had.

What do you like best about your creation?

If you had more time and materials, what would you change?

MATCHBOX CAR ENGINEERING CENTER

Toy cars, like Hot Wheels and Matchbox, have been popular with both boys and girls since they debuted in the 1950s and '60s. Given louder, brighter, more exciting competition, why do these simple toys endure? Perhaps their simplicity is actually a strength. Toy cars are portable, durable, and adaptable.

This center taps into the popularity of Matchbox cars to teach lessons in math, science, engineering, communication, and collaboration. Learners use Matchbox-style tracks to test how different factors affect the distance a toy car travels, incorporating math and science standards. In this collaborative center, learners engage in the engineering process, with its cycle of planning, implementation, reflection, and adjustment.

A major focus is respectful communication among participants. Communication is an essential skill in this center, in education, and in life. The Share Domain features prominently in this center when learners discuss their ideas, listen respectfully, and offer and accept feedback. All facets of communication can be challenging, especially for younger learners. It's easy to become defensive when someone disagrees with your ideas. Also, young learners are often terrible active listeners. Whole-group discussion of what good communication should look like and sound like, with examples, can help facilitate positive collaboration and preempt conflict.

Depending on the amount of materials, this center can accommodate up to six learners working together or in small groups. This center requires flexible tracks that learners can manipulate into loops and easily adjust. Hot Wheels Track Sets work well. If choosing another brand, ensure that the tracks aren't fixed. Consider setting up this center away from the others so learners have enough room to spread out and test their designs. The story area in an elementary school library works well. If the track set includes clamps, these can be affixed to book shelves for more height.

This is a wildly popular center, and learners might become boisterous. Clear expectations and gentle reminders help if the noise level becomes disruptive. Because of this center's popularity, consider keeping a record of learners who have visited the center and rotating until all learners have had a turn. This approach helps ensure fairness and manage learner disappointment.

Decide whether learners will record the measurements on their own sheets or the group will share the responsibility. Individual responses are optimal when using the Matchbox Car Engineering Reflection Sheet (WS 3.18).

Objective

To test basic physics concepts by collaborating on an engineering project.

AASL Standards Framework for Learners

I.C. (Inquire/Share): Learners adapt, communicate, and exchange learning products with others in a cycle that includes:
  2. Providing constructive feedback.
  3. Acting on feedback to improve.

II.C. (Include/Share): Learners exhibit empathy with and tolerance for diverse ideas by:
  1. Engaging in informed conversation and active debate.
  2. Contributing to discussions in which multiple viewpoints on a topic are expressed.

III.D. (Collaborate/Grow): Learners actively participate with others in learning situations by:
  1. Actively contributing to group discussions.
  2. Recognizing learning as a social responsibility.

V.C.3. (Explore/Share): Learners engage with the learning community by collaboratively identifying innovative solutions to a challenge or problem.

Content Areas
- Mathematics
- Science

Lesson Duration
20–40 minutes

Materials
- Matchbox Car Engineering Learner Directions (WS 3.16)
- Matchbox Car Engineering Sheet (WS 3.17)
- Matchbox Car Engineering Reflection Sheet (WS 3.18)
- Matchbox cars, tracks, and connectors
- Yardstick or tape measure
- Pencils

Educator Preparation
1. Purchase materials and find suitable storage.
2. Make a double-sided copy of the Matchbox Car Engineering Learner Directions (WS 3.16) on card stock.
3. Make copies of the Matchbox Car Engineering Sheet (WS 3.17) and the Matchbox Car Engineering Reflection Sheet (WS 3.18).
4. Pre-teach the behavioral expectations and rules for this center. One useful rule is that each learner must immediately retrieve the car after sending it down the track. This stipulation helps prevent car loss and safety issues.

5. Consider discussing basic concepts related to science experiments and investigations, such as the need to repeat the same experiment many times before trusting the results because they can vary widely. Factors that affect results in this investigation may include the amount of force applied when sending the car down the tracks, different tester techniques, and user error.
6. Decide on the best location for the center.

Learner Steps

Partner

1. Learners begin by thinking about how they will set up the tracks.
2. Next, they share and listen to ideas with the group before building.
3. Learners work together to build a set of straight tracks.
4. Then they send a car down the tracks and measure how far the car travels beyond the end of the track using a yardstick or tape measure, recording the data on the Matchbox Car Engineering Sheet (WS 3.17).
5. Before altering their design, learners pause to predict the ways in which raising the height of the track starting point might change the distance the car travels.
6. Learners add height to their design, retest, and record the data.
7. Next, learners create a track that includes one loop, following the previous steps to test their design, and eventually add a second or bigger loop.
8. Finally, learners complete the Matchbox Car Engineering Reflection Sheet (WS 3.18). This review is more beneficial if done individually.

 TROUBLESHOOTING

1. The Matchbox Car Engineering center can take longer to clean up than others. Consider having learners begin 5 minutes before learners in the other centers.
2. If including a retractable tape measure, demonstrate how to safely use it to prevent injury.
3. Getting a car to successfully navigate the looped track may take some trial and error. Be prepared to offer advice if learners are becoming overly frustrated.

Modifications

Younger learners or those struggling with fine motor skills may need help assembling the course at first. Often the collaborative aspect of this center offers enough support, but the school librarian should periodically monitor this center and intercede when necessary to minimize learner frustrations. Other scaffolds are to

- include a ruler with only one unit of measurement and circle the appropriate unit on the Matchbox Car Engineering Sheet (WS 3.17),
- allow learners to draw responses on the Matchbox Car Engineering Reflection Sheet (WS 3.18), or
- eliminate the looped track version, focusing instead on learners increasing the height several times on the straight track or lengthening the track run.

Extensions

Advanced learners can design more elaborate tests to demonstrate complex concepts such as kinetic and potential energy, velocity, friction, and acceleration.

MATCHBOX CAR ENGINEERING LEARNER DIRECTIONS

Task: To collaborate and reflect on an engineering design project.

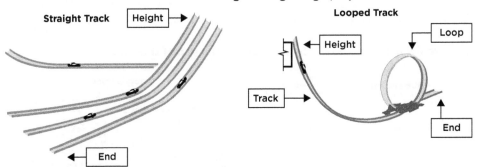

Steps
Straight Tracks

1. Think about how you will set up the tracks.
2. Share and listen to ideas with your group.
3. Work together to build a set of straight tracks.
4. Send a car down the tracks.
5. Measure how far the car travels beyond the end of the track.
6. Record your answers on the Matchbox Car Engineering Sheet.

Raised-Height Straight Tracks

7. Predict how raising the height of the track starting point will change how far the car travels.
8. Share your ideas with your group.
9. Add to your design, making the tracks higher.
10. Repeat steps 4–6.

One-Loop Track

11. Create a track that includes one loop.
12. Send a car down the track.
13. Measure how far the car travels beyond the end of the track. If the car falls off the loop, make changes to the design and retest.
14. Record your answers on the Matchbox Car Engineering Sheet.

Two-Loop (or Larger Loop) Track

15. Predict how adding a second loop or making the first loop bigger will change the distance the car travels.
16. Share your ideas with your group.
17. Change your design.
18. Repeat steps 12–14.
19. Complete the Matchbox Car Engineering Reflection Sheet.
20. Clean up.

MATCHBOX CAR ENGINEERING SHEET

Name _____   Class _____

Measure the distance the car travels beyond the end of the track.

1. How far did the car travel? (Start measuring at the end of the last track.) _____ inches _____ centimeters	1. How far did the car travel? (Start measuring at the end of the last track.) _____ inches _____ centimeters
2. After making the starting point higher, how far did the car travel? _____ inches _____ centimeters	2. After adding a second loop or making the loop bigger, how far did the car travel? _____ inches _____ centimeters
3. Was there a difference?	3. Was there a difference?
4. If yes, what do you think caused the change?	4. If yes, what do you think caused the change?

WORKSHEET 3.18

MATCHBOX CAR ENGINEERING REFLECTION SHEET

Name   Class

What did you learn from this activity?

What problems did you have?

How did you solve these problems?

What would you change next time?

CONSTRUCTION CENTER

The Construction center is by far the most popular and in many ways the simplest. From an early age most children have an innate desire to build. LEGOs and blocks appeal far beyond the primary years, providing opportunities to express creativity, work on fine motor skills, and relieve stress. Learners also work on resiliency when their designs don't cooperate. LEGOs, K'NEX, and magnetic tiles seem to induce quieter, more Zen-like atmospheres, whereas the KEVA Plank and block centers, which topple more easily, periodically erupt in excitement.

Construction lends itself to multiple centers such as LEGO, KEVA Planks, Giant KEVA Foam Planks, K'NEX, magnetic tiles, and blocks. It's well worth the initial investment because most of the materials are basically indestructible. Consider limiting a LEGO Construction center to bricks only. This limitation places the focus on building the structure and differentiates the learning center from the LEGO Story center.

The school librarian could set a daily challenge at the center, but learners often are most creative when left to explore. Some learners will decide to collaborate without prompting. At the end, each learner should complete a Construction Reflection Sheet (WS 3.19). The act of reflection also helps legitimize Construction centers for critics who view them as "just play." For more in-depth discussion of this topic, refer to the section on play in chapter 1.

Learners at this center almost always want to share their creations with others. Encouraging them to do so provides practice in communication and gives them an audience. It also helps lessen feelings of disappointment when they have to dismantle their creations. Photographing the work is another way to validate and preserve learners' efforts.

Objective

To express creativity and practice resiliency through building.

AASL Standards Framework for Learners

V.B.2. (Explore/Create): Learners construct new knowledge by persisting through self-directed pursuits by tinkering and making.

V.D.1. (Explore/Grow): Learners develop through experience and reflection by iteratively responding to challenges.

Content Areas

- Art
- English/Language Arts
- Science
- Technology

Lesson Duration
10–45 minutes

Materials
- Construction Reflection Sheet (WS 3.19)
- LEGO bricks and plates
- KEVA Planks
- Giant KEVA Foam Planks
- K'NEX
- Magnetic tiles
- Any other building materials such as blocks
- Marbles (2–3) to use with KEVA Planks
- Pencils
- Camera or tablet (optional)

Educator Preparation
1. Purchase the materials.
2. Find suitable containers or use the originals for storage.
3. Make several copies of the Construction Reflection Sheet (WS 3.19).
4. If setting specific challenges, create the scenarios or directions.

 TROUBLESHOOTING

1. Before introducing Construction centers, remind learners that they need to put all the materials back when finished so that other classes can use them. This procedure helps keep materials from walking away.
2. Keep the marbles separate from the KEVA Planks so learners must request them from the school librarian and then return them. Otherwise the marbles may get lost.

Learner Steps

Individual
1. If a challenge is set, learners begin by reading and thinking about the task.
2. Learners rarely need to plan when free-building. If they want to, they can do so on the back of the Construction Reflection Sheet (WS 3.19). This step may be necessary with a fixed challenge.
3. Next, learners build, naturally reassessing and adjusting as needed.

4. When finished, learners should complete the Construction Reflection Sheet (WS 3.19) and share their creations if possible.
5. Finally, learners dismantle their creations.

Partner

Often learners will decide to work together in this center. Encourage them to share and listen to ideas equally. When disagreements occur, suggest ways to help learners work through them.

CONSTRUCTION REFLECTION SHEET

Name_____   Class_____

What did you build?

What materials did you use?

What do you like best about your creation?

If you worked with a partner, how did you collaborate?

FAIRY-TALE CHALLENGE CENTER

Cinderella, Goldilocks and the Three Bears, Rapunzel, Snow White, Beauty and the Beast, Jack and the Beanstalk—it's not a coincidence that these fairy tales have stood the test of time. Many have even been made and remade into classic Disney movies.

Fairy tales, as a genre, are part of the curriculum for most elementary school grades. These universal stories offer lessons in dealing with conflict, handling disappointment, and overcoming obstacles. They're also good texts to use when teaching story elements such as character, setting, plot, conflict, and resolution.

This center links reading with engineering. Learners read a common fairy tale and then identify the problem and possible solutions. The Fairy-Tale Challenge Cards (WS 3.23) set a specific task for each story. This task may or may not match the learner-generated problem or solution. Learners have the option of pursuing their own solutions. This option encourages independent, higher level thought and helps accommodate more advanced learners.

Most of the fun lies in building, but if time is limited, learners may not progress beyond reading the fairy tale and planning a solution. If possible, allow eager learners to work in this center for more than one session. In-process work can be stored on top of bookshelves if other storage space is limited. Such works-in-progress often make interesting displays.

This center could be used as a whole-group multilesson project with learners working individually or in small groups. It might also be an opportunity to collaborate with classroom educators.

Dedicating specific copies of the fairy tales that do not circulate is important. Providing props such as a "Goldilocks" doll and a "tower" for Rapunzel helps learners size their designs accordingly. A blank Fairy-Tale Challenge Card (WS 3.23) is included so that school librarians can substitute other fairy tales or folktales from their collection.

Objective

To design and build an object that solves a problem after reading and analyzing a fairy tale.

AASL Standards Framework for Learners

V.A.1. (Explore/Think): Learners develop and satisfy personal curiosity by reading widely and deeply in multiple formats and write and create for a variety of purposes.

V.B. (Explore/Create): Learners construct new knowledge by:

 1. Problem solving through cycles of design, implementation, and reflection.
 2. Persisting through self-directed pursuits by tinkering and making.

Content Areas
- English/Language Arts
- Science

Lesson Duration
20–45 minutes

Materials
- Fairy-Tale Challenge Learner Directions (WS 3.20)
- Fairy-Tale Challenge Planning Sheet (WS 3.21)
- Fairy-Tale Challenge Reflection Sheet (WS 3.22)
- Fairy-Tale Challenge Cards (WS 3.23)
- Copies of the following fairy tales: *Goldilocks and the Three Bears* (suggested versions: James Marshall or Jan Brett); *Rapunzel* (suggested version: Paul O. Zelinsky); *Jack and the Beanstalk* (suggested version: Steven Kellogg); and others
- Pencils
- Consumable building materials such as recycled cardboard, boxes, and paper
- Scissors
- Glue
- Tape
- Staplers
- Ruler
- Doll, tower, and beanstalk (optional)
- Laptop, tablet, or similar device to allow some learners to listen to the story (optional)
- Headphones (optional)

Educator Preparation
1. Purchase or pull copies of the fairy tales.
2. Gather building materials and tools.
3. Copy the Fairy-Tale Challenge Cards (WS 3.23) on card stock and laminate if possible. Cut to separate the cards.
4. Make several copies of the Fairy-Tale Challenge Learner Directions (WS 3.20), Fairy-Tale Challenge Planning Sheet (WS 3.21), and the Fairy-Tale Challenge Reflection Sheet (WS 3.22).

Learner Steps

Individual
1. Learners read the fairy tale and are instructed to think about the problem in the story.

2. Learners fill in the Fairy-Tale Challenge Planning Sheet (WS 3.21) and think of ways to solve the problem.
3. If time allows, learners complete the task set on the Fairy-Tale Challenge Card (WS 3.23) or build their own design, adapting and changing their idea as needed.
4. When finished, learners complete the Fairy-Tale Challenge Reflection Sheet (WS 3.22) and share their design if possible.

Modifications

To accommodate learners needing more support, the school librarian can

- use read-aloud versions of the stories,
- allow students to draw rather than write their ideas,
- identify the problem beforehand and write it for the learner,
- encourage partner work, or
- break the activity into multiple sessions.

Distance Learning

Post one Fairy-Tale Challenge (WS 3.23) at a time online and list suggested recyclable materials to use. Include a link to an online version of the appropriate fairy tale for learners to access. Upload the Fairy-Tale Challenge Planning Sheet (WS 3.21) and the Fairy-Tale Challenge Reflection Sheet (WS 3.22). Encourage learners to photograph and share their creations. The photos can be posted on the school library website, Google Classroom, or similar venue with learner permission.

Extensions

Advanced learners can be challenged to explain how their design solution might change the story.

FAIRY-TALE CHALLENGE LEARNER DIRECTIONS

Task: To design and build a solution to a fairy-tale problem.

Steps

1. Read the story.

2. Think about the problem in the story.

3. Write your answers on the Fairy-Tale Challenge Planning Sheet.

4. Think of a way to solve this problem. Describe your solution on the sheet, and draw a sketch of it.

5. Read the Fairy-Tale Challenge Card for your story. Does the task match your problem and solution?

6. If you have time, you may choose to build your design or complete the task on the card. Use the back of the Fairy-Tale Challenge Planning Sheet if you need to sketch another plan.

7. Complete the Fairy-Tale Challenge Reflection Sheet.

8. Share your design if possible.

FAIRY-TALE CHALLENGE PLANNING SHEET

Name _____   Class _____

Fairy Tale

Problem

Solution

Draw your idea below.

WORKSHEET 3.22

FAIRY-TALE CHALLENGE REFLECTION SHEET

Name _____   Class _____

What fairy tale did you read?

What did you design or build?

What do you like best about your creation?

If you had more materials and time, what would you change?

WORKSHEET 3.23

FAIRY-TALE CHALLENGE CARDS

FAIRY TALE: *Goldilocks and the Three Bears*
Task: To build a just-right chair for Goldilocks

FAIRY TALE: *Rapunzel*
Task: To build something to help Rapunzel escape from the tower without using her hair

---

FAIRY TALE: *Jack and the Beanstalk*
Task: To build something to prevent the giant from climbing down the beanstalk so Jack doesn't have to chop it down

---

FAIRY TALE:
Task:

CHAPTER 4

Technology Centers

Technology, especially during distance learning, has become an essential part of education whether you like it or not. Reading, creating, and presenting online are more important than ever. One of AASL's Common Beliefs is that "information technologies must be appropriately integrated and equitably available" (AASL 2018, 13). What better place to do so than the school library where resources are shared and everyone has access?

This chapter includes four centers—Mini Green Screen, Video Book Review, Book Trailer, and LEGO Story—that move learning with information technologies beyond using computers for research. The centers integrate art, English/language arts, and technology with the *AASL Standards Framework for Learners*. Technology is used as a tool for learners to create and share ideas, engaging with all six AASL Shared Foundations and four Domains.

In two of the centers (Video Book Review and Book Trailer), learners engage in "recalling . . . background knowledge" (AASL 2018, Learner I.A.2.) as they choose books for the center. This Competency may seem fairly simple, but it can be difficult for learners to identify a book or series they know well enough to review. Remembering and finding the book are just the first steps. All four centers require learners to create "products that illustrate learning" (AASL 2018, Learner I.B.3.). The product is set, but the learners need to create the content.

Each center encourages collaboration, providing the opportunity to give and receive feedback and to practice communication skills and empathy. Collaboration is a skill that most learners need to practice continually. Compromising, listening when a partner disagrees, and accepting constructive criticism can be difficult for many learners. The technology centers offer fun, creative activities for practicing these skills. Each center could also be an opportunity to collaborate with classroom and other educators by turning the activities into projects that learners work on over a series of weeks in both the classroom and school library.

Finally, one of the most important and long-lasting benefits of these centers involves the Share Domain. It's important to find ways for learners to share their finished products with a wider audience. Videos can be shared by including them on the school's news show or posting them on the school library's web page with the learner's permission. Another idea is to link videos to QR codes posted in the school library, allowing learners and educators to watch the Video Book Reviews and Book Trailers when looking for books using a QR code reader. This public sharing opportunity will make more learners interested in visiting the technology centers and creating videos of their own to share.

MINI GREEN SCREEN CENTER

Who wants to make a movie? Most learners love being behind or in front of the camera. Using green screen technology ups the cool factor.

This center addresses a variety of AASL and content-area standards by turning learners into filmmakers. Learners use premade characters or make their own to tell a story or create a documentary. A fun addition is to personalize the center with school-specific characters, including color pictures of staff. Pre-teaching how to use the technology and showing examples of short narrative and informative videos are helpful. However, be prepared to reteach and continue to support learners as they work on their videos.

This center is collaborative by necessity, requiring at least two participants—one to present and one to film. The best number of learners is two to four. The technology can be difficult for younger learners to navigate on their own. Even more advanced learners may need to spend time learning how to use it. Be prepared to step in often. Designating a few learners in each class who are "green screen experts" to help with future productions is empowering. Because of the learning curve, consider allowing learners to work in this center for multiple sessions. If continuing the project, it's best for the school librarian to hold on to the sheets for safekeeping. Having more than one Mini Green Screen studio available opens up this center to more learners.

Writing a script before filming is preferable but not mandatory because it is time-consuming. A simple list of events may work just as well. Learners with limited time may want to jump right into filming and use premade characters. Those with more time, and the possibility of continuing their project in the future, may create a script and characters. The majority of learners will want to film and refilm until they're satisfied with the result. When finished, learners can consider ways to share their videos with other classmates or the learning community. For many learners, this part brings the most enjoyment.

This center could easily present an opportunity for collaboration with a classroom educator. For example, if the second grade is studying animals, consider having students make animal documentaries. Learners could research an animal, write a script, create characters, film, edit, and share their documentaries.

Objective
To create a video that tells a story or gives information using green screen technology.

AASL Standards Framework for Learners
I.B.3. (Inquire/Create): Learners engage with new knowledge by following a process that includes generating products that illustrate learning.

II.D.2. (Include/Grow): Learners demonstrate empathy and equity in knowledge building within the global learning community by demonstrating interest in other perspectives during learning activities.

III.B.1. (Collaborate/Create): Learners participate in personal, social, and intellectual networks by using a variety of communication tools and resources.

V.A.1. (Explore/Think): Learners develop and satisfy personal curiosity by reading widely and deeply in multiple formats and write and create for a variety of purposes.

Content Areas

- Art
- English/Language Arts
- Technology

Lesson Duration

20–45 minutes

Materials

- Mini Green Screen Learner Directions (WS 4.1)
- Mini Green Screen Planning Sheet (WS 4.2)
- Mini Green Screen Character Cards (WS 4.3)
- Mini Green Screen Reflection Sheet (WS 4.4)
- Tablet or similar device (with a green screen app such as Green Screen by Do Ink, a 2019 AASL Best App for Teaching and Learning, and with background photos preloaded)
- Pizza box (large size is best)
- Green paper (standard construction paper works) or paint
- Rulers or sticks (covered in green paper or painted)
- Green gloves (optional)
- Masking tape or Blu Tack adhesive
- Characters (laminated)
- Blank paper
- Scissors
- Crayons, colored pencils, or markers
- Pencils

Educator Preparation

1. Download a green screen app to a tablet or other device and learn how to use it.
2. Download a variety of free use images to the tablet camera roll to use as background scenes.

3. Get a large pizza box (local restaurants are usually happy to give you an extra for free).
4. Cover the inside of the pizza box completely with green paper or paint.
5. Cover 10 or more rulers or sticks with green paper or paint.
6. Print the Mini Green Screen Character Cards (WS 4.3) on card stock and laminate them. (Because these cards are in black and white, consider having some learners color them before laminating.) Cut the characters out, leaving little white space.
7. Take photos of school staff. Size the photos to fit with other characters and print in color on card stock. Laminate and cut them out.
8. Copy the Mini Green Screen Learner Directions (WS 4.1) on card stock and laminate.
9. Make several copies of the Mini Green Screen Planning Sheet (WS 4.2) and the Mini Green Screen Reflection Sheet (WS 4.4).
10. Consider introducing the green screen app to the whole group.
11. Decide how and where to share and store the videos.

 TROUBLESHOOTING

Videos and photos saved only to a tablet's camera roll are vulnerable and can easily be deleted. Protect these by stressing the importance of respecting the work of others. Frequently downloading finished videos to a safe place also helps.

Learner Steps

Partner

1. Learners are directed to look at the character choices and think about what kind of video they want to make. They have the option of making their own characters.
2. Next, learners discuss ideas with their partners and use the Mini Green Screen Planning Sheet (WS 4.2) to sketch out the video, creating a script or timeline of events, or both.
3. Learners need to select a background image and may ask for assistance in downloading alternative images if none suits their needs.
4. Next, learners prepare to film by using masking tape or Blu Tack to attach a green ruler or stick horizontally on one side of each character. If green gloves are available, learners may use them instead to insert characters into the scene.
5. Learners should practice once or twice before filming.
6. Finally, learners film and watch the video, refilming until happy with the result.
7. At the end, learner teams share their videos if possible, clean up, and complete the Mini Green Screen Reflection Sheet (WS 4.4).

Modifications

Some learners may need more support in this center because using a tablet and a green screen app can be complicated. The school librarian can help by

- providing a ready-made script to use,
- limiting the choice of characters,
- giving consistent hands-on assistance, or
- filming the video and providing needed tech support.

Extensions

Green screen technology can be used on a larger scale, with learners delivering news shows, weather reports, or other presentations. All that's needed is a green background and an empty wall. It can even be used during distance learning.

Although many school libraries produce daily news shows, not every learner is able to take part. The news crew is often limited to older learners, sometimes on a rotating basis. This arrangement means that younger learners may have to wait years to use this cool feature. This center gives all curious newscasters the chance to experiment.

MINI GREEN SCREEN LEARNER DIRECTIONS

Task: To create a video that tells a story or gives information using green screen technology.

Steps

1. Look at the character choices and think about what kind of video you want to make. A narrative film tells a story. An informative film gives facts.
   a. Discuss your ideas with your partners and listen to their ideas.
   b. You can make your own characters if you want.

2. Use the Mini Green Screen Planning Sheet (WS 4.2) to write down your ideas and sketch out the video, creating a script, a timeline of events, or both. Although this planning sheet will help you organize your ideas, it may be difficult to read from when filming.

3. Select a background image for your video. If none of the available options work, ask the school librarian if it's possible to download others.

4. Attach the characters to the green rulers or sticks with masking tape or Blu Tack horizontally on one side of each character. This handle will make it easier for you to insert characters into the scene without your hand showing. Remember to put the tape or adhesive behind the character so it doesn't show in the video.

5. Practice once or twice before filming.

6. Film and then watch the video.

7. Redo until you're happy with the result.

8. Share with the school librarian and others if possible.

9. Clean up, carefully removing the tape or Blu Tack from the characters and green rulers or sticks.

10. Complete the Mini Green Screen Reflection Sheet (WS 4.4).

MINI GREEN SCREEN PLANNING SHEET

Name _____   Class _____

Use the space below to plan your video. Think about the characters you will use and what each one will say. List the events or facts in order. If you need more space, continue on the back.

Characters (Who is in the video?)	Descriptions (What's important about each character?)

Events (What happens?) or Facts	Dialogue (What do the characters say?)

MINI GREEN SCREEN CHARACTER CARDS

MINI GREEN SCREEN CHARACTER CARDS (*cont'd*)

MINI GREEN SCREEN REFLECTION SHEET

Name _____   Class _____

What type of video did you create? (Narrative or Informative?)

What problems did you have?

How did you solve these problems?

What do you like best about your video?

What would you change next time?

VIDEO BOOK REVIEW CENTER

Everyone loves a good book review. So many books, so little time! When faced with the question of what to read next, turning to a friend or classmate can be a huge help.

Although this center relies on technology, it's fairly simple and straightforward. Even young learners usually need little support when filming. It's also an efficient way to address the AASL Standards, integrating five of the six Shared Foundations. Learners choose a book they've read to recommend. The Video Book Review Planning Sheet (WS 4.6) provides a template to follow. Each review contains basic information about the book and the reason the presenter is recommending it. This center would be a good starting point for learners before moving on to the Book Trailer center, which is more open ended and technically challenging.

Beforehand designate a quiet place, such as the school library office, for learners to film their videos. Even low-level background noise can be distracting. Pre-teaching tips for good-quality presentations is helpful. These tips are listed in the Video Book Review Learner Directions (WS 4.5).

Objective

To demonstrate communication skills by creating a video review that summarizes and evaluates a book.

AASL Standards Framework for Learners

I.A.2. (Inquire/Think): Learners display curiosity and initiative by recalling prior and background knowledge as context for new meaning.

I.B.3. (Inquire/Create): Learners engage with new knowledge by following a process that includes generating products that illustrate learning.

I.C. (Inquire/Share): Learners adapt, communicate, and exchange learning products with others in a cycle that includes:

> 1. Interacting with content presented by others.
> 4. Sharing products with an authentic audience.

III.B.1. (Collaborate/Create): Learners participate in personal, social, and intellectual networks by using a variety of communication tools and resources.

IV.A.3. (Curate/Think): Learners act on an information need by making critical choices about information sources to use.

V.A.1. (Explore/Think): Learners develop and satisfy personal curiosity by reading widely and deeply in multiple formats and write and create for a variety of purposes.

VI.D.1. (Engage/Grow): Learners engage with information to extend personal learning by personalizing their use of information and information technologies.

Content Areas

- English/Language Arts
- Technology

Lesson Duration

15–30 minutes

Materials

- Video Book Review Learner Directions (WS 4.5)
- Video Book Review Planning Sheet (WS 4.6)
- Tablet or video camera
- Pencils

Educator Preparation

1. Copy the Video Book Review Learner Directions (WS 4.5) on card stock and laminate.
2. Make several copies of the Video Book Review Planning Sheet (WS 4.6).
3. Decide whether learners will check out the book they are using in the review or simply use it in the school library and return it to the shelf when finished.
4. Plan how and where learners will share their videos.
5. Consider any necessary modifications.

Learner Steps

Individual

1. Learners find books in the school library that they've read and would like to recommend.
2. Next, learners read the summary on the back or inside front cover and flip through the pages to help them remember what happens in their books.
3. Learners use the Video Book Review Planning Sheet (WS 4.6) to take notes.
4. Learners should find someone to help film their review. If no one is available, they can set up the tablet at a table to film themselves.
5. Learners should practice a few times before filming and review the tips for presenters and videographers.
6. Finally, learners will film, watch, and redo as needed. They should save only the final, "good" version, deleting all previous versions.
7. Learners end by sharing their video if possible.

Partner

Although each learner will present an individual book review, there is an opportunity for collaboration. The videographer should film and offer feedback.

Modifications

English learners and others may need extra support in this center. The school librarian may

- remind the learner where to find the title and author,
- provide sentence stems (for example, "This book is about _____ who _____." "I like this book because it is _____."),
- create a word bank with pictures for commonly used adjectives (*funny, scary, exciting, sweet*).

Distance Learning

Post the Video Book Review Learner Directions (WS 4.5) and the Video Book Review Planning Sheet (4.6) online. Learners can review books they own, or they can review e-books from the school library collection or from sites such as myON and Tumble-Books. Learners can record their Video Book Reviews using Flipgrid (a 2017 AASL Best App for Teaching and Learning) or a similar tool and share them with the school librarian and classmates online.

VIDEO BOOK REVIEW LEARNER DIRECTIONS

Task: To create a video recommending a book.

Steps

1. Find a book in the school library that you've read and would like to recommend.

2. Read the summary on the back or inside front cover and flip through the pages to help you remember what happens in the book.

3. Use the Video Book Review Planning Sheet (WS 4.6) to plan what you will say.

4. If you're the only one working at this center, find someone who will film for you. If no one is available, set up the tablet (or video camera) at a table and prepare to film yourself sitting down.

5. Practice what you will say a few times before filming.

6. Hold the book in front of you, so viewers can see the cover. Begin by saying your name. Then include all other parts (title, author, short summary, reason for recommending).

7. Follow the tips below when filming.

8. Watch your video and redo it if necessary.

9. Keep only the final "good" video. Delete all other versions of your video only. Do not delete videos saved by other students on the camera roll.

10. Share your video.

Tips for Presenters	Tips for Videographers
1. Practice several times.	1. Stay in one place. Don't fidget.
2. Speak to the camera. This will help you make eye contact. Smile!	2. Film the presenter from the waist up.
3. Don't read from the paper.	3. Give a countdown (3-2-1) before filming so the presenter knows when to start.
4. Speak loudly, slowly, and clearly.	4. Keep the camera as steady as possible. If you're shaking the camera, the video will look shaky. Locking your elbows at your sides or resting them on a table can help.
5. Hold the book in front of you with the cover showing. If you want to share illustrations from inside the book, mark the pages with a sticky notes in advance to make them easy to find.	5. Stop filming after the presenter stops talking.
6. Try not to fidget or move around. Sitting down helps if you find it hard to stay still.	

VIDEO BOOK REVIEW PLANNING SHEET

Name _____   Class _____

Use the space below to plan your video. This sheet will help you organize your ideas. Do not read from the paper when filming. Include all the parts below in order. If you need more space, continue on the back.

Title	
Author	
What is the book about? (Two or three sentences about the main characters, where the story happens, and what happens. Don't give away the ending or any surprises!)	
Why are you recommending this book? (Why should someone else read it? Is it funny? Is it scary? Does it have great illustrations?)	

BOOK TRAILER CENTER

For some people, one of the best parts of going to a movie theater is watching the trailers. They preview upcoming movies, highlighting the most exciting parts, and give you something to look forward to. Book trailers, like movie trailers, are short video clips that are meant to grab viewers' attention and persuade them to read the book rather than watch the movie.

In this center learners have another chance to become filmmakers. Although similar to the Video Book Review, this center involves more advanced technical skills and will most likely require multiple sessions for quality work. The emphasis is on advertising a specific book or series. Learners may choose from a variety of tools, such as iMovie, Sock Puppets, LEGO Movie Maker, or similar apps. Sock Puppets and LEGO Movie Maker are fun, especially for younger learners, but they have limitations such as choice of characters and scenes. It may sound counterintuitive, but when using iMovie, learners should choose to create a new movie instead of a trailer. The trailer template is complicated and may include unnecessary sections that are hard to delete.

Whole-group discussion of the persuasive techniques used in advertising would be a great way to introduce this center. You can tie in lessons on media literacy and digital citizenship. Don't forget to address the issue of copyright and ethical use of information because learners may want to use images from the Internet.

Drum up excitement by demonstrating the different tools and showing professional book trailers. Seeing examples of book trailers really helps learners understand the difference between a book review and a book trailer. If it's not possible to provide a whole-group lesson, have a few book trailers available for learners to watch as needed.

Learners may work individually or in small groups. If learners are collaborating, remind them to communicate respectfully. Consider having learners, especially those needing more support, work in the Video Book Review center before moving on to this one.

Sharing their book trailers is often the most exciting part of the process. Consider ways for learners to present to an authentic audience. As with the Video Book Reviews, QR codes could be posted near relevant books in the school library and linked to trailers. You might also consider collaborating with the public library in your community to see if staff members might be interested in sharing the reviews as well.

Objective

To advertise a book or series of books by creating a book trailer.

AASL Standards Framework for Learners

I.B.3. (Inquire/Create): Learners engage with new knowledge by following a process that includes generating products that illustrate learning.

I.C.4. (Inquire/Share): Learners adapt, communicate, and exchange learning products with others in a cycle that includes sharing products with an authentic audience.

IV.C.2. (Curate/Share): Learners exchange information resources within and beyond their learning community by contributing to collaboratively constructed information sites by ethically using and reproducing others' work.

V.A.1. (Explore/Think): Learners develop and satisfy personal curiosity by reading widely and deeply in multiple formats and write and create for a variety of purposes.

VI.C. (Engage/Share): Learners responsibly, ethically, and legally share new information with a global community by:

1. Sharing information resources in accordance with modification, reuse, and remix policies.
2. Disseminating new knowledge through means appropriate for the intended audience.

VI.D.1. (Engage/Grow): Learners engage with information to extend personal learning by personalizing their use of information and information technologies.

Content Areas

- English/Language Arts
- Technology

Lesson Duration

30–60 minutes

Materials

- Book Trailer Learner Directions (WS 4.7)
- Book Trailer Planning Sheet (WS 4.8)
- Tablet or similar device (loaded with iMovie or similar; Sock Puppets; LEGO Movie Maker, a 2015 AASL Best App for Teaching and Learning; and other presentation tools)
- Sample book trailers
- LEGO characters (optional)
- Craft materials to make characters (optional)
- Pencils

Educator Preparation

1. Download presentation tools to a tablet or similar device.
2. Find examples of short, high-quality book trailers.

3. Consider introducing the center to the whole class at once, demonstrating the different presentation tools and showing the sample book trailers. Use this opportunity to discuss how to ethically find and use images from the Internet.
4. Discuss the purpose of book trailers, explaining that they are persuasive in nature and meant to advertise books. Emphasize that learners are not creating a book review.
5. Copy and laminate the Book Trailer Learner Directions (WS 4.7).
6. Make several double-sided copies of the Book Trailer Planning Sheet (WS 4.8).
7. Designate a quiet area for learners to film their trailer if necessary.

Learner Steps

Individual

1. Learners choose a book or series to highlight. It helps if learners have copies of the books for reference and possibly to use in the trailer.
2. Before planning, learners should decide which presentation tool to use and think about how to grab viewers' attention.
3. Next, learners use the Book Trailer Planning Sheet (WS 4.8) to map out the scenes and make any props they need. If using an image from the Internet, learners are directed to ask for help to cite the source.
4. Learners should set up the scene and practice several times before they start filming.
5. Learners then film their trailer, watch the video, and redo if necessary.
6. Learners are instructed to keep only the final "good" video, deleting all other versions of their video only.
7. The final step is to share the video. This may happen at a later time.

Partner

When working in pairs or small groups (a maximum of four learners is recommended), learners should follow the same steps, integrating discussion throughout.

Modifications

Learners requiring more support should be encouraged to use one of the simpler presentation tools such as Sock Puppets or LEGO Movie Maker and to work with a partner.

BOOK TRAILER LEARNER DIRECTIONS

Task: To create a video advertising a book or series of books.

Steps
1. If working with a partner, make sure you share and listen to ideas throughout the project in a respectful way.
2. Choose your subject. This can be a specific book or a whole series of books that you're familiar with. You will be making a trailer to advertise a book or series. This project is different than a book review.
3. Decide which presentation tool to use and how you will grab viewers' attention. Will you use photo images, illustrations, LEGOs, 3-D models you make, or live action video?
4. Use the Book Trailer Planning Sheet (WS 4.8) to map out the action. The first side asks for basic information. The second side shows a storyboard on which you can draw each scene and add what you will say. This storyboard will be helpful when you are filming.
5. Make or find any props you need (characters, photos). If using an image from the Internet, make sure it's free to use and cite it. Ask your school librarian for help with this.
6. Practice several times before filming.
7. Film. Watch your video and redo it if necessary.
8. Keep only the final "good" video. Delete all other versions of your video only. Do not delete other videos saved on the camera roll.
9. Share your video.

Your book trailer must contain the following:
- Title (If you are advertising a series, give the name of the series, not the names of individual books.)
- Author
- Citation information for any images borrowed from the Internet (Ask your school librarian about this.)
- Your name

BOOK TRAILER PLANNING SHEET

Name _____   Class _____

Use the spaces below to plan your video. This information will help you organize your ideas. Use the storyboard on the next page to map out each part.

Title (If you are advertising a series, say or list the name of the series.)	
Author (If the books in a series have different authors, state this.)	
What is the book or series about (main characters, setting, problem, genre)? **Why should readers choose this book or series?** (A good trailer is interesting and entertaining. It convinces viewers to choose that book or series by telling just a bit about it. Don't give away the ending or any surprises!)	
What presentation tool (app) will you use?	
What props will you use to create your trailer (photos, 3-D characters, LEGOs, drawings, live actors)?	

Use this storyboard to plan your trailer. You can draw each scene in order and add words. Use blank paper if you need more space.

1	2	3
4	5	6
7	8	9
10	11	12

LEGO STORY CENTER

"The name 'LEGO' is an abbreviation of the two Danish words 'leg godt,' meaning 'play well'" (LEGO Group, n.d.). Very fitting indeed! These versatile plastic bricks have been captivating learners for more than one hundred years for good reason.

This center could easily fit in the maker, literacy, and technology centers because it combines the skills of all three. However, the emphasis here is on creating and sharing a narrative video. Learners use LEGO bricks, characters, and props to build a scene before filming themselves narrating the story. This center is one of the most popular, with learners wanting to visit again and again.

It's easy to become engrossed in building and forget to leave time for the most important part of the activity—narrating and filming the story. After all, LEGOs are fun! Setting a timer or giving verbal reminders is usually necessary. It's a good idea to leave ten to fifteen minutes for filming, viewing, and sharing or posting learners' videos so those last steps aren't rushed. This timing also depends on the number of available recording devices and quiet spaces. Allow more time if learners have to share these.

Before introducing this center, model the difference between telling a story and playing. Learners should also be familiar with using a tablet or video camera. Emphasize proper filming techniques, such as keeping hands out of the frame and holding the camera steady. Have learners practice and consider the advantages of filming from different angles. Front facing or aerial view? Keeping the camera fixed or rotating it to show another side? Rotation is easier to do if working with a partner.

Learners can write notes about the story arc beforehand, but this process takes time and should only be used to help them organize their thoughts. They should not attempt to read from these notes as a script when filming the story. The emphasis is on storytelling, which is an advanced skill. It can be difficult to create a story while you're telling it. Some learners may choose to retell a familiar story, which is also a great way to promote collaboration as part of an English/language arts educator's lesson.

This center requires an initial but worthwhile investment. It's often possible to buy whole sets of LEGOs that include characters like community helpers (firefighter, doctor, police officer). Supplement and replenish this center with yard sale finds or community donations.

Making a video and sharing it with others can make it easier for those who are reluctant to dismantle their scenes at the end. Consider how and where learners can save and post their videos for others to watch. One idea is to make the LEGO Story videos available in another center where learners can view and respond to them.

Objective
To film and narrate a story depicted through a LEGO scene.

AASL Standards Framework for Learners

I.B.3. (Inquire/Create): Learners engage with new knowledge by following a process that includes generating products that illustrate learning.

1.C.4. (Inquire/Share): Learners adapt, communicate, and exchange learning products with others in a cycle that includes sharing products with an authentic audience.

V.A.1. (Explore/Think): Learners develop and satisfy personal curiosity by reading widely and deeply in multiple formats and write and create for a variety of purposes.

V.B.2. (Explore/Create): Learners construct new knowledge by persisting through self-directed pursuits by tinkering and making.

Content Areas

- Art
- English/Language Arts
- Technology

Lesson Duration

30–45 minutes

Materials

- LEGO Story Learner Directions (WS 4.9)
- LEGOs, including characters and props
- LEGO base plates (1 per learner)
- Tablet or video camera

Educator Preparation

1. Copy the LEGO Story Learner Direction (WS 4.9) on card stock and laminate.
2. Gather materials.
3. Introduce the center and model necessary lessons.

Learner Steps

Individual

1. Learners are asked to think about a story they want to tell and to create a scene for that story on one of the base plates using LEGOs.
2. When finished building the scene, learners will make notes and practice telling their story, thinking about these questions:
    - How does the story begin?
    - Who are the characters in the story?
    - What is the problem?
    - How is the problem solved?
    - How does the story end?

3. Learners are instructed to consider how they will film the scene (angle, fixed, or moving) and to practice first.
4. Next, learners set up their video camera or tablet in a quiet spot and film the scene as they narrate and act out the story with the LEGO characters, deleting and redoing as needed.
5. When finished, learners watch their video and share it with a classmate. If posting the video online, learners will need to give their story a title and perhaps write a short description. If there's not enough time, this part could be done in a later session.
6. Learners end by dismantling their scenes.

Partner

Although this center is better suited to an individual activity, learners often choose to work together and join their plates to create a larger scene. Do not discourage this organic form of collaboration. Instead, ensure that both partners are sharing ideas and taking part in the storytelling.

 TROUBLESHOOTING

1. To prevent theft, place this center close to the circulation desk or in a prominent position. Also, tell learners, especially young ones, directly that the materials must be put back in the box at the end because this center is for everyone in the school to share.
2. Some learners interpret "take everything apart" to include taking the limbs and heads off the LEGO people. It can be very difficult to reattach the arms, even for adults! Unless you want to spend a lot of time performing LEGO surgery, continually remind learners not to take the characters apart.

Modifications

Younger learners may need assistance when filming their stories. Retelling a familiar story may also be helpful if a learner is struggling to create an original story.

REFERENCE

LEGO Group. n.d. "About Us" [The LEGO Group History]. Accessed July 13, 2020. https://www.lego.com/en-us/aboutus/lego-group/the-lego-group-history.

LEGO STORY LEARNER DIRECTIONS

Task: To build a scene using LEGOs and create a narrated film of the story.

Steps

1. Think about a story you want to tell.

2. Create a scene for that story on one of the base plates using LEGOs.

3. When finished, practice telling your story. Think about the following questions and take notes on a blank paper if you want:
   - How does the story begin?
   - Who are the characters in the story?
   - What is the problem?
   - How is the problem solved?
   - How does the story end?

4. Think about how you will film the story. What's the best angle? Try viewing the scene from different angles: front facing, from above, from the side. Will you keep the camera fixed or move it while you film?

5. If possible, set up the tablet or video camera on a table to minimize shaking. If you shake the camera when filming, the video won't be very clear.

6. Practice before you start filming.

7. Your voice will be recorded, but you won't be seen in the video. Try not to put your hands in front of the camera too often because they will block the screen. Remember to speak slowly, loudly, and clearly. Begin filming.

8. If you make a mistake, stop the recording and start over.

9. Erase each mistake video before refilming. Otherwise you might delete the wrong version later.

10. When finished, watch the video. If you're happy with it, share it with a classmate.

11. If posting the video online, give it a title and write a short description. Don't forget to include your name!

12. Dismantle your LEGO scene and clean up for the next learner.

CHAPTER 5

Literacy Centers

iteracy centers may seem the most logical to those expecting a more traditional school library experience. It makes sense if you think school library = books = reading = English/language arts. Although all the literacy centers require learners to read, write, or speak, they also integrate art, science, and technology content-area standards with the AASL Standards.

Poetry, something learners often groan about, is a big focus. Three centers—Blackout Poetry, Word Drawing, and Book Spine Poetry—address poetry writing in fun ways that make it less intimidating. In these centers "learners engage with new knowledge by following a process that includes generating products that illustrate learning" (AASL 2018, Learner I.B.3.). Learners are introduced to different types of poetry and then apply what they've learned by writing their own poems.

In each of the literacy centers, learners "write and create for a variety of purposes" (AASL 2018, Learner V.A.1.). This is similar to the "illustrate learning" Competency in the Inquire Shared Foundation in that something is created. However, the Explore Shared Foundation refers to using a growth mindset, one in which learners are open to new, challenging experiences.

To immerse learners in poetry, consider setting up all the poetry centers for three consecutive weeks and cycling learners through them. This approach gives them practice in writing different types of poetry. The fourth week could be set aside for learners to share their favorite poems. The finished products would make a great display.

Most of the literacy centers are relatively open ended and offer natural differentiation. For these reasons, modifications and extensions are not always included. After being introduced to each center, most learners should be pretty self-sufficient.

MINI-ANAGRAM CENTER

This center focuses on word play. It's super easy to set up, requires minimal supplies, and can accommodate several learners at once.

An anagram is a word, phrase, or sentence made by reordering all the letters in another word, phrase, or sentence. A mini-anagram uses only some of the letters in a word. Forming anagrams involves reading, spelling, vocabulary, and pattern recognition. The school librarian can either choose a challenge word for the day or let learners choose their own words from those provided. Learners manipulate the letters to form as many different words as possible. Even young learners can participate in this activity.

This center can be an individual challenge or a competition to see who can find the most words. Words can be one letter long, but proper nouns and abbreviations do not count. Other options include using a timer and having more than one round of challenge words. If table space is limited, consider having learners use clipboards. The school librarian should decide what to do with the finished sheets: save them or let learners take them.

This activity could easily be adapted for online use during distance learning or used to fill the last few minutes of class if a lesson finishes early.

Objective
To form as many words as possible by recombining the letters in a challenge word.

AASL Standards Framework for Learners
I.A.2. (Inquire/Think): Learners display curiosity and initiative by recalling prior and background knowledge as context for new meaning.

V.A.1. (Explore/Think): Learners develop and satisfy personal curiosity by reading widely and deeply in multiple formats and write and create for a variety of purposes.

Content Area
- English/Language Arts

Lesson Duration
10–20 minutes

Materials
- Mini-anagram Learner Directions (WS 5.1)
- Mini-anagram Sheet (WS 5.2)

- Mini-anagram Challenge Words (WS 5.3)
- Folder, large envelope, or bin to store materials
- Dictionary (optional)
- Clipboards (optional)
- Timer (optional)
- Pencils

Educator Preparation

1. Copy and laminate the Mini-anagram Learner Directions (WS 5.1) and the Mini-anagram Challenge Words (WS 5.3).
2. Cut the challenge words apart and separate into bundles.
3. Make several copies of the Mini-anagram Sheet (WS 5.2).
4. Store items in a folder, large envelope, or bin.
5. Model the activity.

Learner Steps

Individual

1. Learners write their name, class, and the challenge word on their Mini-anagram Sheet (WS 5.2).
2. Next, learners look at the challenge word and think about different ways to combine the letters. They can use as many or as few of the letters as they like to make different words. Proper nouns and abbreviations may not be used.
3. Learners are instructed to write down as many words as possible in the time given.
4. Finally, learners count the number of words they made and write the total at the bottom of the sheet.

Partner

If learners decide to make it a competition, when finished they count up the number of words created to determine the winner. Another option is to have learners read their words to the other participants so learners can cross-check each other for accuracy.

Modifications

Consider the following ways to accommodate learners needing more support:

- Choose simpler challenge words.
- Provide a simple dictionary (with pictures if possible) for learners to use.
- Fill in the sheet beforehand with some words, leaving some letters blank.
- Provide pictures of some of the words that can be made from the challenge word.

Distance Learning

Post the Mini-anagram Learner Directions (WS 5.1) online with three to five challenge words for learners to choose from. This can be used as an asynchronous individual activity or with a whole class during synchronous instruction using an online whiteboard or Padlet (2013 AASL Best App for Teaching and Learning). At the end, learners can also type their answers in the chat box.

Extensions

Ask learners to use all the words on their sheet to write a few sentences or a paragraph.

MINI-ANAGRAM LEARNER DIRECTIONS

Task: To use the letters in the challenge word in any order to form as many words as possible.

Example:

Challenge Word	Words You Can Make			
plant	a	pan	nap	pant
	an	pat	tap	tan
	at	apt	pal	lap
	ant	plan		

Steps

1. Write your name, class, and the challenge word on your Mini-anagram Sheet (WS 5.2).

2. Look at the challenge word and think about different ways to combine the letters.

3. You can use as many or as few of the letters as you like to make different words.

4. You cannot use proper nouns (words that would be capitalized, like names) or abbreviations (short forms of words).

5. Write down as many words as you can make in the time given.

6. At the end, if competing against other learners, take turns reading your lists.

7. Count the number of words you made and write the total at the bottom of the sheet.

MINI-ANAGRAM SHEET

Name _____   Class _____

Challenge Word _____

Write your words on the lines below.

_____	_____	_____
_____	_____	_____
_____	_____	_____
_____	_____	_____
_____	_____	_____
_____	_____	_____
_____	_____	_____
_____	_____	_____
_____	_____	_____
_____	_____	_____
_____	_____	_____
_____	_____	_____
_____	_____	_____

How many words did you make? _____

MINI-ANAGRAM CHALLENGE WORDS

Copy the words below on card stock and laminate before cutting them out. Use the blank spaces to add your own words.

library	library	library	library
inventor	inventor	inventor	inventor
holiday	holiday	holiday	holiday
education	education	education	education
adventure	adventure	adventure	adventure
creation	creation	creation	creation
anagram	anagram	anagram	anagram
pleasing	pleasing	pleasing	pleasing
sandwich	sandwich	sandwich	sandwich
flashlight	flashlight	flashlight	flashlight
together	together	together	together
dollhouse	dollhouse	dollhouse	dollhouse
teacher	teacher	teacher	teacher

BLACKOUT POETRY CENTER

Blackout poetry looks an awful lot like a redacted government document with all the top secret or sensitive bits covered up. All those black lines give the page and the poem a kind of harsh beauty. Most learners enjoy the act of crossing out words on a printed page because it can feel like breaking a rule. It's like taking a bath with your clothes on or eating spaghetti with your hands. Breaking a small rule, one that doesn't hurt anyone, can help unleash creativity.

This feeling of freedom can be very important when writing poetry, part of the English/language arts curriculum in most grades. Learners are asked to read, analyze, and write poetry, which can be difficult for many. This center makes poetry writing accessible and fun with built-in scaffolds. Blackout poetry removes the pressure of creating original work.

Learners use pages from discarded books and magazines to create poems by blacking out unwanted words with markers. The remaining words on the page form a poem. Remind learners that the way a poem sounds is as important as its meaning. Encourage them to read the words out loud before blacking anything out. Learners should give each poem a title, mount the poem on colored paper, and add illustrations for display. If time allows, learners can share their poems by reading them aloud.

Create a few examples to keep with the center materials for reference. Modeling the process and using the activity with the whole class before introducing the center is helpful. Consider displaying finished work in the school library.

Objective
To create a poem from words on a printed page.

AASL Standards Framework for Learners
I.B.3. (Inquire/Create): Learners engage with new knowledge by following a process that includes generating products that illustrate learning.

V.A.1. (Explore/Think): Learners develop and satisfy personal curiosity by reading widely and deeply in multiple formats and write and create for a variety of purposes.

Content Areas
- Art
- English/Language Arts

Lesson Duration
10–20 minutes

Materials

- Blackout Poetry Learner Directions (WS 5.4)
- Pages from discarded books and magazines
- Construction or colored paper
- Black markers (thick and thin)
- Glue, tape, or stapler
- Scissors
- Markers, colored pencils, or crayons
- Rulers (optional)
- Pencils

Educator Preparation

1. Copy the Blackout Poetry Learner Directions (WS 5.4) on card stock and laminate.
2. Gather discarded books and magazines. To save time, cut or tear out pages and keep them in a folder to prevent creasing.
3. Gather all other materials.
4. Model how to create a blackout poem.

Learner Steps

Individual

1. Learners choose a page and read it through once.
2. Learners read the page through a second time, using a pencil to circle the words they want to keep.
3. Before blacking anything out, learners should read the page through again, focusing on the circled words this time.
4. Next, learners make changes, adding words or editing the form of a word if needed.
5. Using a black marker, learners cross out all the unwanted words on the page. Instruct them to use a thick marker to black out whole lines at once if possible. Some learners may want to use a ruler to keep the lines neat.
6. Learners give their poem a title and write their name on the front of the paper.
7. Before backing the poem with colored paper, learners can trim the edges with scissors.
8. The final, optional, step is to illustrate the frame or blank parts of the paper.
9. Learners can share their poems by reading them out loud if possible.

Modifications

Distance Learning

Post the Blackout Poetry Learner Directions (WS 5.4) online. With adult permission, learners can use pages from newspapers, magazines, or old books. The school librarian could also scan and post pages from books for learners to black out digitally. It would be interesting to read all the different poems that can be created from the same page of text. Encourage learners to share their poems in a safe forum online.

BLACKOUT POETRY LEARNER DIRECTIONS

Task: To create a poem from words on a printed page.

Steps

1. Choose a page from the folder.

2. Read it through once.

3. Read it a second time and use a pencil to circle the words you want to keep.

4. Read it through out loud, reading only the circled words this time. Do you like how it sounds?

5. Make changes if needed. You can add words or edit the form of a word (for example, make it plural) to make your poem sound better.

6. Black out all the unwanted words with a marker. It's best to use long, straight lines rather than scribble. It looks neater. You can use a ruler to make this process easier.

7. Give the poem a title and write your name on the front of the paper.

8. Trim the edges with scissors if needed.

9. Glue, tape, or staple the page to a larger sized colored paper to make a frame.

10. Illustrate the frame or blank parts of the page if you like.

11. If time allows, read your poem to a classmate.

WORD DRAWING CENTER

Learners of all ages enjoy cutting, pasting, and making collages. The widespread popularity of scrapbooking proves this. Arranging words and pictures to convey a message or preserve a memory can be incredibly satisfying.

This center combines art with poetry writing in a low-stress, inclusive activity. One way to get learners excited about writing poetry is to show them it doesn't have to be complicated or serious. Like the Blackout Poetry center, Word Drawing helps ease the anxiety associated with creating original poetry.

A poem uses words to create an image in the mind of the reader. A concrete poem enlists the shape the words take on the page to help convey meaning. In the Word Drawing center, learners create concrete poems by cutting and pasting words from discarded books and magazines into shape templates. Learners can add texture and color to their poems with basic art supplies.

Consider introducing this center after a unit on poetry. Providing books of poetry, including concrete poetry, for learners to reference would be helpful. However, be sure to clearly mark the school library books so learners do not mistakenly cut them up. The finished products make lovely displays.

Objective
To create a concrete poem.

AASL Standards Framework for Learners
I.B.3. (Inquire/Create): Learners engage with new knowledge by following a process that includes generating products that illustrate learning.
V.A.1. (Explore/Think): Learners develop and satisfy personal curiosity by reading widely and deeply in multiple formats and write and create for a variety of purposes.

Content Areas
- Art
- English/Language Arts

Lesson Duration
10–25 minutes

Materials
- Word Drawing Learner Directions (WS 5.5)
- Word Drawing Template (WS 5.6A–WS 5.6J)
- Poetry books (including concrete poetry)

- Dictionary, thesaurus (optional)
- Discarded books and magazines
- Glue
- Scissors
- Markers, colored pencils, or crayons
- Colored paper, ribbon, feathers, and other decorative items
- Pencils

Educator Preparation

1. Copy the Word Drawing Learner Directions (WS 5.5) on card stock and laminate.
2. Make several copies of each Word Drawing Template (WS 5.6A–WS 5.6J).
3. Gather poetry book examples.
4. Gather discarded books and magazines and decide how to clearly differentiate these from the example books.
5. Gather art supplies and other materials.

Learner Steps

Individual

1. Learners choose preprinted templates or create their own shape on the blank template (WS 5.6J).
2. Learners are instructed to think about words that describe the object and to look at examples in poetry books for ideas.
3. Next, learners flip through discarded books and magazines to find words to use in their poem. Learners are also given the option of cutting out separate letters to make words or writing their own words in the template.
4. Learners arrange the words inside the shape, read the poem out loud, and make any changes before gluing down the words.
5. Learners can add illustrations and other decorations to their poem.
6. If time allows at the end, learners should read their poem to a classmate.

Modifications

Distance Learning

Post the Word Drawing Learner Directions (WS 5.5) and the templates online. Learners can choose a template and print it out or re-create the shape on a blank page at home. With adult permission, learners can cut words from pages in newspapers, magazines, or old books. They can also write their own words. Encourage learners to share their poems in a safe forum online.

WORD DRAWING LEARNER DIRECTIONS

Task: To create a concrete or shape poem.

Concrete poems are also called *shape* or *pattern poems* because the words are displayed in a shape that adds to the poem's meaning.

Steps

1. Choose a template (WS 5.6A–5.6J).

2. Think about what words you might use to describe the object. Look at examples in poetry books for ideas.

3. Look through the discarded books and magazines (not the poetry books) for words to use in your poem. If you can't find whole words, you can cut out separate letters to make the words. You can also write your own words.

4. Arrange the words inside the shape.

5. Read the poem out loud.

6. Make all the changes you want to the words or the arrangement of words before gluing them down.

7. Add illustrations and other decorations if you like.

8. If time allows, read your poem to a classmate.

WORD DRAWING TEMPLATE: BUTTERFLY

Name _____   Class _____

WORD DRAWING TEMPLATE: FLOWER

Name _____   Class _____

WORKSHEET 5.6C

WORD DRAWING TEMPLATE: HEART

Name _____ Class _____

WORD DRAWING TEMPLATE: SNOWFLAKE

Name _____   Class _____

WORD DRAWING TEMPLATE: SUN

Name _____ Class _____

WORD DRAWING TEMPLATE: WAVE

Name _____   Class _____

WORKSHEET 5.6G

WORD DRAWING TEMPLATE: DOG

Name   Class

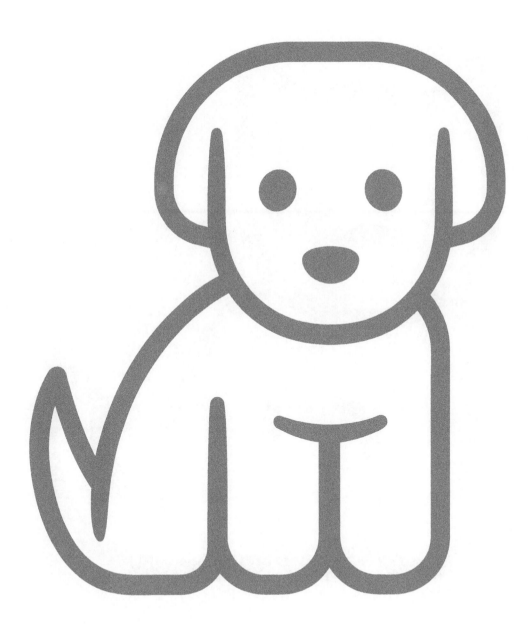

WORD DRAWING TEMPLATE: CAT

Name _____   Class _____

WORD DRAWING TEMPLATE: STAR

Name _____   Class _____

WORD DRAWING TEMPLATE: BLANK

Name _____   Class _____

Draw your own outline below for your concrete poem.

PHOTO-BOOK CENTER

Optical illusion books are often hugely popular in school libraries, rarely getting reshelved before being checked out again. It's easy to find a group of learners huddled over one of these books oohing and ahhing.

This center relies on a type of optical illusion book called photicular from the nonfiction series by Dan Kainen (Workman Publishing). These books contain images that appear to move when the pages are turned, so it looks like you're watching a 3-D video. The books in this series focus on animals from specific habitats or regions. Each introduction explains photicular technology and gives tips for using the book. One page of factual information about the animal, at roughly a third- to fifth-grade reading level, accompanies each image. Other nonfiction books about animals can be substituted, but then the center loses its wow factor.

A great way to introduce learners to this center and entice them to choose it is to demonstrate how photicular technology works. Be prepared to hear a lot of "wow" and "cool." After selecting a book, learners look through it and choose their favorite animal to focus on. They read the information about that animal and answer questions on the Photo-Book Sheet (WS 5.7). Offering at least four books to choose from ensures that everyone has a choice. Learners often want to borrow these books, so consider purchasing a second set to circulate.

Objective

To use a nonfiction text to answer questions about an animal.

AASL Standards Framework for Learners

I.B.1. (Inquire/Create): Learners engage with new knowledge by following a process that includes using evidence to investigate questions.

IV.B.4. (Curate/Create): Learners gather information appropriate to the task by organizing information by priority, topic, or other systematic scheme.

V.A. (Explore/Think): Learners develop and satisfy personal curiosity by:
1. Reading widely and deeply in multiple formats and write and create for a variety of purposes.
3. Engaging in inquiry-based processes for personal growth.

Content Areas

- English/Language Arts
- Science

Lesson Duration
15–30 minutes

Materials
- Photo-Book Sheet (WS 5.7)
- Photicular books: *Safari; Outback; Dinosaur; Polar; Ocean; Jungle;* and *Wild* by Dan Kainen, or similar books about animals
- Blank paper (for younger learners)
- Pencils

Educator Preparation
1. Make several copies of the Photo-Book Sheet (WS 5.7).
2. Purchase or gather books.

Learner Steps

Individual
1. Learners choose a book and flip through the pages to find their favorite picture.
2. Learners read the information about their animal and answer the questions on the Photo-Book Sheet (WS 5.7).

Modifications
Struggling or new readers can be asked to draw a picture of their favorite animal and copy its name.

PHOTO-BOOK SHEET

Name _____ Class _____

Task: To use a nonfiction text to answer questions about an animal.

Steps
1. Choose a book and flip through the pages.
2. Find your favorite picture and read the information about that animal.
3. Answer the questions below.

What is the title of the book?	
What animal did you choose (name)?	
How big is the animal (size)?	
Where does the animal live (habitat)?	
What does the animal eat (diet)?	
What is one more fact about the animal? (Write your answer as a sentence.)	
Why did you choose this animal? (Write your answer as a sentence.)	

BOOK SPINE POETRY CENTER

Title, author, front cover, back cover, spine. Often one of the first school library lessons for kindergartners is to identify the parts of a book. They sometimes find it funny that both people and books have spines.

This center focuses on poetry, often with hilarious results. Book spine poems are created by stacking books and reading the titles on their spines from top to bottom. Learners scour the library shelves searching for titles that will act as lines of poetry. The resulting poems can be silly or serious.

Provide shelf markers or sticky notes to mark book locations. At the end of the activity, learners are asked to return their books to the shelves. This saves the school librarian from having to do it. If learners are unfamiliar with shelf markers, demonstrate correct usage. Beforehand, ensure that learners can identify the spine of a book. Model the activity by creating a book spine poem. Consider photographing and copying the poem to include as an example for the center.

Learners can alter the titles by covering or replacing words with small pieces of paper if needed. Although no minimum or maximum number of books is set, an ideal amount is three to ten books. To document the poem, learners can either copy it down on the Book Spine Poetry Sheet (WS 5.9) or photograph it. If time allows, encourage learners to share their poems with a classmate. Printing out color images of the poems would make an interesting display.

Objective
To create a poem using the spines of books.

AASL Standards Framework for Learners
I.B.3. (Inquire/Create): Learners engage with new knowledge by following a process that includes generating products that illustrate learning.

IV.B.1. (Curate/Create): Learners gather information appropriate to the task by seeking a variety of sources.

V.A.1. (Explore/Think): Learners develop and satisfy personal curiosity by reading widely and deeply in multiple formats and write and create for a variety of purposes.

Content Area
- English/Language Arts

Lesson Duration
15–25 minutes

Materials
- Book Spine Poetry Learner Directions (WS 5.8)
- Book Spine Poetry Sheet (WS 5.9)
- Library books
- Shelf markers or sticky notes
- Tablet or camera (optional)
- Pencils

Educator Preparation
1. Copy the Book Spine Poetry Learner Directions (WS 5.8) on card stock and laminate.
2. Make several copies of the Book Spine Poetry Sheet (WS 5.9).
3. Gather other materials.
4. Model the activity.
5. Consider any necessary modifications.

Learner Steps

Individual
1. Learners are instructed to take shelf markers or sticky notes with them as they browse the school library shelves looking for interesting titles.
2. When learners find a title to use, they take the book off the shelf, leaving a shelf marker or sticky note in its place.
3. After finding all the books they need, learners stack them one on top of the other in the same direction with the spines facing the same way.
4. Next, learners read their poem out loud and make any changes that are needed before reading it through again.
5. Finally, learners copy their poem on the Book Spine Poetry Sheet (WS 5.9), take a picture of it, or do both.
6. If time allows, learners should share their poem with a classmate.

Partner
Although this center is more suited to individual activity, some learners may prefer to work with a partner. If so, they can follow the same steps, integrating discussion throughout. Another option is for partners to take turns selecting the titles. This approach increases the challenge because learners must build off their partner's previous line of poetry.

Modifications

Struggling readers may find this activity difficult. Encourage these students to work with a partner, choose books with simple titles, and use fewer books.

Distance Learning

Post the Book Spine Poetry Learner Directions (WS 5.8) online. Learners will need to use books found at home to create poems. Encourage learners to share their poems in a safe forum online.

Extensions

An interesting way to extend learning is to use an app like Voki, Tellagami, or ChatterPix (a 2019 AASL Best App for Teaching and Learning) to present the poems. Learners can upload an image of their book spine poem to use as the background and then record themselves reading their poem. Some apps let them create an avatar. Consider how learners can share these videos with the learning community. One idea is to make the videos available in a center where learners can view and respond to the work of others.

BOOK SPINE POETRY LEARNER DIRECTIONS

Task: To create a book spine poem by stacking books and reading the titles on their spines from top to bottom.

Steps

1. Take shelf markers or sticky notes with you and browse the school library shelves. Read the spines looking for interesting titles. Think about how they will sound together. Remember you are writing a poem.

2. If you find a title you want to use, take the book off the shelf, leaving a shelf marker or sticky note in its place. You will have to return the book to the same place afterward.

3. When you have found all the books you want, stack them one on top of the other in the same direction. The spines should all face the same way so they can be read easily.

4. Read through the poem from top to bottom out loud. Each book spine is one line of the poem. How does it sound? Do you want to add or delete anything? Do you need to change part of a title? You can add, delete, or change words within the book spine titles by using sticky notes.

5. Make any changes needed.

6. Read the poem through again.

7. When your poem is finished, copy it on the Book Spine Poetry Sheet (WS 5.9), take a picture of it, or do both.

8. If time allows, read your poem to a classmate.

BOOK SPINE POETRY SHEET

Name _____   Class _____

Copy your book spine poem below and give it a title. If you need more space, add another page..

Title _____

_____

_____

_____

_____

_____

_____

_____

_____

_____

_____

_____

GRAMMAR HUNT CENTER

The days of diagramming sentences may be long gone, but grammar is still a necessary part of daily life for most people. You might not be asked to identify parts of speech in a sentence, but you certainly need to be able to use them correctly. Numerous articles complain that many college students and graduates have poor writing skills. Why is this, and how do we fix it?

Grammar is still part of most English/language arts instruction. Like poetry, it's often a less popular topic. Let's face it—grammar lessons can be pretty dull. This center aims to change that. It focuses on the four major parts of speech. Learners search discarded books and magazines to find a specific part of speech in word and picture form. They cut these out and paste them in the appropriate Grammar Hunt Sheet (WS 5.11A–WS 5.11E) to create a collage. If including a picture, they must label it with the corresponding word. For example, if they paste a picture of a running dog on the noun sheet, they should write the word *dog* next to the image. That same picture of a running dog pasted on the verb sheet would be labeled *run*.

Whether learners are working individually or with a partner, this activity includes some collaboration. At the end, learners must ask a classmate to check their sheet. This is a chance to share their work.

Although each part of speech is defined, pre-teaching and reviewing these beforehand with the whole group is helpful. Tearing pages out of books and magazines helps save time. Having learners rotate through each part of speech center over four weeks ensures that they've covered them all. Use the blank Grammar Hunt Sheet (WS 5.11E) to add other parts of speech.

Objective

To identify specific parts of speech and use them in a collage.

AASL Standards Framework for Learners

I.A.2. (Inquire/Think): Learners display curiosity and initiative by recalling prior and background knowledge as context for new meaning.

I.B.3. (Inquire/Create): Learners engage with new knowledge by following a process that includes generating products that illustrate learning.

Content Areas

- Art
- English/Language Arts

Lesson Duration
15–20 minutes

Materials
- Grammar Hunt Learner Directions (WS 5.10)
- Grammar Hunt Sheet: Nouns (WS 5.11A)
- Grammar Hunt Sheet: Verbs (WS 5.11B)
- Grammar Hunt Sheet: Adjectives (WS 5.11C)
- Grammar Hunt Sheet: Adverbs (WS 5.11D)
- Grammar Hunt Sheet: _____ (WS 5.11E)
- Discarded books and magazines
- Scissors
- Glue
- Pencils

Educator Preparation
1. Copy the Grammar Hunt Learner Directions (WS 5.10) on card stock and laminate.
2. Make several copies of each Grammar Hunt Sheet (WS 5.11A–WS 5.11E).
3. Gather all materials.
4. Consider tearing or cutting pages from the discarded books and magazines.
5. Model the activity and review parts of speech.

Learner Steps

Individual
1. Learners choose a Grammar Hunt Sheet and read the definition of the part of speech selected.
2. Next, learners look through discarded books and magazines to find words and pictures that match this part of speech.
3. Then learners cut out the words and pictures and paste them on the template in a visually pleasing way to create a collage. If using a picture, learners must write the word near it and can add words of their own as well.
4. When finished, learners should ask a classmate to check their work.

Partner
Although this center is meant to be an individual activity, learners may choose to work with a partner. If so, they should follow the same steps sharing ideas throughout.

Modifications

Learners needing support can

- work with a partner,
- focus on identifying pictures that match the part of speech, and
- focus on nouns or verbs.

Distance Learning

Post the Grammar Hunt Learner Directions (WS 5.10) and the Grammar Hunt Sheets (WS 5.11A–WS 5.11E) online. You can post one at a time or allow learners to select one from all the worksheets. Learners can print the Grammar Hunt Sheet to use or simply use a blank paper. With adult permission, learners can use pages from newspapers, magazines, or old books. They may also write their own words. Encourage learners to share their collages in a safe forum online. Good companion texts include the Words Are CATegorical series by Brian P. Cleary and the Grammar All-Stars: The Parts of Speech series by Doris Fisher.

Extensions

Advanced learners can be asked to sort the words and pictures into categories and list these on the back of the page. Learners should explain the rationale behind each category.

GRAMMAR HUNT LEARNER DIRECTIONS

Task: To identify specific parts of speech and use them in a collage.

Steps

1. Choose a Grammar Hunt Sheet and read the definition of the part of speech selected.

2. Look through the books and magazines provided to find words and pictures that match this part of speech.

3. Cut out the words and pictures and paste them on the template in a visually pleasing way to create a collage.

4. If using a picture, write the word near it.

5. You may add words of your own as well.

6. When finished, ask a classmate to check your work.

GRAMMAR HUNT SHEET: NOUNS

Name _____   Class _____

Noun. A person, place, or thing.

Examples: George Washington, pool, New York, dog, tape

Paste your words and pictures inside the box. Arrange them into a collage.

WORKSHEET 5.11B

GRAMMAR HUNT SHEET: VERBS

Name   Class

Verb. A word that tells about an action or state of being. It's what the noun is doing.

Examples: Run, play, sleeps, are, see

Paste your words and pictures inside the box. Arrange them into a collage.

GRAMMAR HUNT SHEET: ADJECTIVES

Name _____ Class _____

Adjective. A word that describes or tells something about a noun.

Examples: Old, pretty, seven, hairy, nice

Paste your words and pictures inside the box. Arrange them into a collage.

GRAMMAR HUNT SHEET: ADVERBS

Name _____   Class _____

Adverb. A word that describes a verb, adjective, or other adverb.

Examples: Quickly, carefully, hardly, very

Paste your words and pictures inside the box. Arrange them into a collage.

GRAMMAR HUNT SHEET: _____

Name _____ Class _____

Definition:

Examples:

Paste your words and pictures inside the box. Arrange them into a collage.

CHAPTER 6

Library and Research Skills Centers

Books, research, and the Dewey Decimal Classification system. For many, these are what a traditional school library brings to mind. The Library and Research Skills centers should be familiar to most school librarians because they include typical library activities.

This chapter includes five centers in which learners practice a variety of skills to help them navigate the school library and become proficient researchers. One of the most important research skills is curation—"collecting, organizing, and sharing resources" (AASL 2018, Learner IV). Four of the five centers require learners to apply skills from this Shared Foundation. Being able to find, evaluate, and use appropriate sources—essential for academic success—can be challenging for learners. Repeated practice can help tremendously.

The Resource Investigation and Database Exploration centers show learners that research and reference materials can be interesting and fun to use. When faced with a research project, learners often resort to Google because it's quick and easy. Once learners become familiar and comfortable with more credible resources, such as databases, they'll be more likely to use these in the future.

Not only will learners become better independent researchers, they might even be able to help out in the school library. The Endangered Books center asks learners to help vet books to weed from the collection by offering written recommendations. The Book Cart center offers practice in shelving books. This center can make it easier for learners to find books in most libraries by making them familiar with Dewey organization.

ENDANGERED BOOKS CENTER

Every school library has books that don't circulate often. The reason isn't always clear. Does the book look old or uninviting? Is its shelf location less than ideal? Are readers wowed by more popular series and simply need a booktalk to introduce them to a fantastic story?

Weeding is an ongoing and necessary part of school library curation. Sometimes it can be hard to decide what to weed and what to keep. It's obvious if books have torn pages, broken bindings, or outdated information, but what about award-winning titles that continue to sit on the shelf? For these books, learner input can be a huge help.

In this center, learners engage in high-level critical thinking while helping to curate the school library collection. Begin by gathering books under consideration for weeding in a crate or cart. Perhaps pick ones that haven't been checked out in three or four years. Everybody/Picture books or short books are best because learners must read them before helping to decide their fate.

Most learners really enjoy being asked their opinion and take the role seriously. It can be a huge self-esteem boost. After choosing a book from the Endangered Books cart or crate and reading it, learners evaluate the book's merit and answer a series of questions on the Endangered Books Recommendation Sheet (WS 6.2). School librarians can use these recommendations when deciding whether to discard, reorder, or keep the books.

Objective

To analyze a book and build a case for its inclusion in or removal from the school library collection.

AASL Standards Framework for Learners

I.D.4. (Inquire/Grow): Learners participate in an ongoing inquiry-based process by using reflection to guide informed decisions.

IV.B.3. (Curate/Create): Learners gather information appropriate to the task by systematically questioning and assessing the validity and accuracy of information.

IV.D. (Curate/Grow): Learners select and organize information for a variety of audiences by:

1. Performing ongoing analysis of and reflection on the quality, usefulness, and accuracy of curated resources.
3. Openly communicating curation processes for others to use, interpret, and validate.

V.A.1. (Explore/Think): Learners develop and satisfy personal curiosity by reading widely and deeply in multiple formats and write and create for a variety of purposes.

Content Area

- English/Language Arts

Lesson Duration

15–30 minutes

Materials

- Endangered Books Learner Directions (WS 6.1)
- Endangered Books Recommendation Sheet (WS 6.2)
- Everybody/Picture books or short books to be weeded
- Pencils

Educator Preparation

1. Gather weeded books in a bin or cart and label it "Endangered Books."
2. Copy the Endangered Books Learner Directions (WS 6.1) on card stock and laminate.
3. Make several copies of the Endangered Books Recommendation Sheet (WS 6.2).

Learner Steps

Individual

1. Learners choose an endangered book and read it.
2. As they read, they are instructed to think about possible reasons why the book hasn't been checked out in a while.
3. Finally, they answer the questions on the Endangered Books Recommendation Sheet (WS 6.2).

Modifications

Learners needing more support could work with a partner, reading the book and answering the questions together.

Extensions

If time allows, partners can read and evaluate the same two books. At the end, they can discuss and debate their recommendations.

ENDANGERED BOOKS LEARNER DIRECTIONS

Help! These books haven't been checked out in a long time, and they are in danger of becoming extinct. You can decide the fate of one of these school library books.

Task: To decide the fate of a school library book and write a recommendation.

Steps

1. Choose an endangered book and read it.
2. As you read, think about possible reasons why it hasn't been checked out in a while.
3. Answer the questions on the Endangered Books Recommendation Sheet.

WORKSHEET 6.2

ENDANGERED BOOKS RECOMMENDATION SHEET

Name _____   Class _____

Title	
Author	
Why do you think this book hasn't been checked out? (Check all that apply.)	❑ Old looking ❑ Bad cover ❑ Smells bad ❑ Old or incorrect information ❑ Too many of the same title ❑ Not interesting ❑ Other:
What year was the book published? (Look on the copyright page in the front of the book.)	
What is the best thing about this book?	
What should we do with this book?	❑ Keep it. ❑ Discard it. ❑ Buy a new copy of it.
Explain your recommendation. (You can continue on the back of this sheet if you need more space.)	

BOOK CART CENTER

All those school library books aren't going to shelve themselves, unfortunately. Like laundry, checking in, sorting, and shelving books are never-ending tasks for school librarians. Adult volunteers are great but not always available. Learners, trained to shelve books correctly, just may be the answer.

The Book Cart center provides practice in shelving Everybody books—sometimes called Picture or Easy books—and Nonfiction books. Learners gain helpful library skills while working on alphabetical and decimal order. Learners are given a stack of books and tasked with putting them in order using call numbers. They must alphabetize the Everybody books and use decimal order for the Nonfiction books. Ordering decimals is a math skill usually introduced in fourth grade, so this task may be too challenging for younger learners. Consider limiting them to the Everybody books or begin offering this center at the upper elementary grades.

You can either use the Book Cart Labels (WS 6.4) to change the call numbers on discarded books or simply use the existing call numbers. The premade labels correspond to the Book Cart Answer Sheet (WS 6.5), so you will need to create another answer sheet if you are using different call numbers. If you are using the original call numbers, make sure they are all from the same section (Everybody, Fiction, or Nonfiction), or the task may be confusing.

If possible, set up this center using a real book cart. The cart makes the activity more realistic and easier to set up. It can be more fun to have two learners, one on each side of the cart, competing against each other to finish. When they're done and have checked their answers using the Book Cart Answer Sheet (WS 6.5), they can swap sides. If you can't spare a cart, the books can be kept in separate bins and stacked in order on a table or even on an empty shelf in a bookcase.

Objective
To put books in order according to call number.

AASL Standards Framework for Learners
I.A.2. (Inquire/Think): Learners display curiosity and initiative by recalling prior and background knowledge as context for new meaning.

Content Areas
- English/Language Arts
- Mathematics

Lesson Duration
10–20 minutes

Materials

- Book Cart Learner Directions (WS 6.3)
- Book Cart Labels (WS 6.4)
- Book Cart Answer Sheet (WS 6.5)
- Discarded books
- Book cart or bins
- Bookends and bookshelf (optional)
- Alphabet chart (optional)

Educator Preparation

1. Gather discarded books and sort into like categories or relabel using the Book Cart Labels (WS 6.4).
2. Copy the Book Cart Learner Directions (WS 6.3) on card stock and laminate.
3. Copy the Book Cart Answer Sheet (WS 6.5) on card stock and laminate, or create your own answer sheets.
4. Designate where learners will sort the books (book cart, table, or empty book shelf).
5. Review decimal order with learners if necessary.

Learner Steps

Individual

1. Learners read the Book Cart Learner Directions (WS 6.3) and begin putting their stack of books in order (left to right) according to call number.
2. When finished, learners use the Book Cart Answer Sheet (WS 6.5) to check their work.
3. To clean up, learners mix up the order of the books so they're ready for the next learner.

Partner

Encouraging learners to compete against a partner to see who can finish first or get the most correct makes this center more exciting.

Modifications

Limit learners who haven't been introduced to decimal order to sorting Everybody books. Provide an alphabet chart for reference.

Extensions

Learners who have demonstrated a facility with putting books in order can assist in shelving school library books.

BOOK CART LEARNER DIRECTIONS

In 1873 Melvil Dewey developed a system for organizing library books according to topic (Britannica School, n.d.). This system, with some variations, is still used in most libraries today. Books are labeled with call numbers that usually appear on spine labels. Nonfiction books use numbers and the first three letters of the author's last name. Many public and school libraries organize their Fiction and Everybody books according to genre. In this case, it's common to see an E (for Everybody) or an F (for Fiction) and the first three letters of the author's last name on the spine label.

Your school librarian probably uses this system too. Learning how this system works makes it much easier to find specific books in your school library as well as in other libraries you may visit. In the Book Cart Center you'll practice reading call numbers and organizing books by call number.

Task: To put books in order using the Dewey Decimal Classification system.

Steps

1. If given a choice, decide which type of books to organize—Everybody or Nonfiction.

2. Look at a book's call number (on the spine label) and place the book with the spine facing out on the cart or shelf.

3. Continue sorting the rest of the books in alphabetical (Everybody) or decimal (Nonfiction) order, from left to right. If two Nonfiction books have exactly the same call number, use the author's last name to decide which goes first alphabetically.

4. When finished sorting all the books, use the Book Cart Answer Sheet (WS 6.5) to check your work.

5. Clean up, making sure you mix up the book order.

Reference

Britannica School. (n.d.). S.v. "Dewey Decimal Classification." https://school.eb.com/levels/elementary/article/Dewey-Decimal-Classification/626207.

BOOK CART LABELS

Everybody Labels Set 1

E Alb	E And	E Fle	E Hen
E Lea	E Lee	E Pol	E Rex
E Rey	E Van	E Wil	E Win

Everybody Labels Set 2

E Bor	E Bro	E Cap	E Car
E DeP	E Edw	E Mun	E Mur
E Par	E Seu	E Tho	E Yol

(cont'd)

BOOK CART LABELS

Nonfiction Labels Set 1

398.2 Aes	398.2 Mar	428.1 Cle	597.3 Col
597.3 Otf	597.34 Mor	796.323 Leb	796.332 Kop
796.334 Hor	811.008 Ran	811.54 Sil	973.8 Boy

Nonfiction Labels Set 2

398.2 Kel	398.21 Loh	523.43 Sto	523.492 Vog
599 Joh	599.638 Bod	599.756 Gen	629.222 And
629.228 Pie	736.982 Geo	745.5 Nic	994 Hei

WORKSHEET 6.5

BOOK CART ANSWER SHEET

Directions: Find your set below and check your answers.

Everybody Labels Set 1

E	E	E	E	E	E	E	E	E	E	E	E
Alb	And	Fle	Hen	Lea	Lee	Pol	Rex	Rey	Van	Wil	Win

Everybody Labels Set 2

E	E	E	E	E	E	E	E	E	E	E	E
Bor	Bro	Cap	Car	DeP	Edw	Mun	Mur	Par	Seu	Tho	Yol

Nonfiction Labels Set 1

398.2	398.2	428.1	597.3	597.3	597.34
Aes	Mar	Cle	Col	Otf	Mor
796.323	796.332	796.334	811.008	811.54	973.8
Leb	Kop	Hor	Ran	Sil	Boy

Nonfiction Labels Set 2

398.2	398.21	523.43	523.492	599	599.638
Kel	Loh	Sto	Vog	Joh	Bod
599.756	629.222	629.228	736.982	745.5	994
Gen	And	Pie	Geo	Nic	Hei

DATABASE EXPLORATION CENTER

Databases are like Target. When you go to Target, you can buy cereal, books, slippers, towels, and a new bike all in the same place. Databases offer this type of one-stop shopping when you are looking for information. Images, videos, encyclopedia articles, websites, newspapers, and magazines can all be found with one search.

Most school librarians are probably on the same mission—to convince learners to use reliable, credible sources such as databases rather than simply doing a Google search. Databases make a researcher's task so much easier. Educators who went to school in the pre-Internet days, flipping through the *MLA Handbook* to document sources on typewriters, can't understand. Why do learners resist?

The Database Exploration center can help convince learners that databases are their friends. Self-directed exploration makes this activity seem more like play than work. This center is also an efficient way to target the AASL Standards with four of the six Shared Foundations—Inquire, Curate, Explore, and Engage—included. This connection makes sense given that research is at the heart of school library instruction. Learners ask questions, locate and evaluate sources, and, finally, share and cite their findings.

Provide access to several databases if possible so learners are able to make "critical choices about information sources to use" (AASL 2018, Learner IV.A.3.). Some good general databases for elementary learners include Britannica School Elementary, World Book Kids, and PebbleGo/PebbleGo Next. Upper elementary and middle school learners may prefer Britannica School Middle and World Book Student. Consider introducing this center after whole-group lessons on using databases and citing sources. Demonstrate the different features of each database, including videos, images, puzzles, and games.

Decide how learners will document their sources. Full-scale documentation can be confusing for young learners. They might only be asked to write the name of the database. It's important that learners understand the reasons why they need to cite their sources. It's better to start slowly and teach good research habits early rather than wait until third or fourth grade to introduce this concept. Usually by second grade, learners will be able to locate and copy citation information from a database. They may need a demonstration and reminders on where to find it. Many elementary schools use the MLA style, and this is often the default on databases. If your school uses a different style, be sure to explain this to learners beforehand.

If learners prefer to record their answers digitally on a Google Doc or similar, ensure that they are familiar with cutting and pasting. Although it may be difficult to toggle back and forth between pages, this practice makes it easier to insert the citation information.

Objective

To generate and answer questions and cite source information using databases.

AASL Standards Framework for Learners

I.A.1. (Inquire/Think): Learners display curiosity and initiative by formulating questions about a personal interest or a curricular topic.

I.B.1. (Inquire/Create): Learners engage with new knowledge by following a process that includes using evidence to investigate questions.

IV.A. (Curate/Think): Learners act on an information need by:

    2. Identifying possible sources of information.

    3. Making critical choices about information sources to use.

V.C.1. (Explore/Share): Learners engage with the learning community by expressing curiosity about a topic of personal interest or curricular relevance.

VI.A. (Engage/Think): Learners follow ethical and legal guidelines for gathering and using information by:

    1. Responsibly applying information, technology, and media to learning.

    2. Understanding the ethical use of information, technology, and media.

    3. Evaluating information for accuracy, validity, social and cultural context, and appropriateness for need.

VI.B. (Engage/Create): Learners use valid information and reasoned conclusions to make ethical decisions in the creation of knowledge by:

    1. Ethically using and reproducing others' work.

    2. Acknowledging authorship and demonstrating respect for the intellectual property of others.

    3. Including elements in personal-knowledge products that allow others to credit content appropriately.

Content Areas

- English/Language Arts
- Technology

Lesson Duration

20–45 minutes

Materials

- Database Exploration Learner Directions (WS 6.6)
- Database Exploration Sheet (WS 6.7)
- Laptop or tablet (1 per learner)
- Pencils

Educator Preparation

1. Copy the Database Exploration Learner Directions (WS 6.6) on card stock and laminate.
2. Make several copies of the Database Exploration Sheet (WS 6.7).
3. Create and print directions for learners to log on to your school's databases.
4. Teach any necessary introductory lessons.

Learner Steps

Individual

1. Learners follow school-specific directions to log on to a database.
2. Next, learners read and follow the Database Exploration Learner Directions (WS 6.6).
3. Learners are directed to browse the database's different features.
4. Learners are instructed to think of a person, place, or thing they want to know more about and to write it down on the Database Exploration Sheet (WS 6.7).
5. Next, learners write down one to three questions about their topic.
6. Learners type their topic in the search box and then choose an article that seems like a good match and click on it.
7. Learners skim and search the article for answers to their questions and write down the answers.
8. Learners are reminded to cite their information and to ask the school librarian if they need help.
9. If learners can't answer all the questions, they can skip to another article or another database and repeat the steps.

Modifications

Encourage struggling readers and English learners to use the read-aloud and translation features on many databases.

Distance Learning

The school librarian should create an instructional video, step-by-step direction sheet, or slide show to guide learners in accessing databases. Post the Database Exploration Learner Directions (WS 6.6) and the Database Exploration Sheet (WS 6.7) online for asynchronous learning. During synchronous instruction, school librarians can have learners use Google Docs or Slides or Pear Deck (a 2015 AASL Best Website for Teaching and Learning) to record their work. Encourage learners to share their research with classmates online.

Extensions

This activity can be extended by asking learners to create a slide or PowerPoint presentation to share their research with a wider audience. This would also be a good opportunity for the school librarian to collaborate with classroom educators on content-area projects. This center would be a good way for learners to practice quoting, paraphrasing, and citing information.

DATABASE EXPLORATION LEARNER DIRECTIONS

Task: To generate and answer questions and cite source information using databases.

Steps

1. Log on to a database.
2. Browse the different features.
3. Think of a person, place, or thing you want to know more about. Write this down on the Database Exploration Sheet (WS 6.7).
4. Write down one to three questions about your topic. (See below for an example.)
5. Type your topic in the search box and hit Enter. Look at the results. Click on the different types of information. There should be articles, videos, images, magazines, and websites.
6. Choose an article that seems like a good match and click on it. Not all the results will apply. (For example, a search for *lions* might bring up articles about the animal and about the Detroit Lions football team.)
7. Skim and search the article for answers to your questions. When you find an answer, write it down. If you copy right from the article, you need to put the words in quotation marks. (See the following chart for an example.)
8. Now you need to cite your information, or show where it came from. Databases make it easy to find and copy this information. Look for a "cite" or "citation" icon. On some databases this information is listed under Tools. Choose the style (MLA, APA, Chicago) that your school uses. Remember, you can ask the school librarian for help.
9. Copy this information on your Database Exploration Sheet (WS 6.7).
10. Skip to another article if you can't find an answer. Repeat steps 7–9.
11. Once you've exhausted all hits on that database, try a different one. Not every database will have the answer to every question.
12. Repeat steps 5–9 if you are using another database.

Example:

Topic: Lions

Question	Answer	Database Citation (MLA)
What do lions eat?	"Lions eat zebras, warthogs, wildebeests, and gazelles."	"Lions." *Animals.* Capstone, 13 June 2020. www.pebblego.com.
Where do lions live?	Lions live in the grasslands of Asia and Africa.	"Lions." *Animals.* Capstone, 13 June 2020. www.pebblego.com.
How big do lions grow?	Lions can grow as long as 9 or 10 feet and weigh 300–500 pounds.	"Lion." Britannica School, *Encyclopædia Britannica,* 8 Feb. 2020. school.eb.com/levels/elementary/article/lion/353389. Accessed 13 June 2020.

WORKSHEET 6.7

DATABASE EXPLORATION SHEET

Name _____   Class _____

Topic: _____

Question	Answer	Database Citation (See the Database Exploration Learner Directions [WS 6.6] for an example.)

RESOURCE INVESTIGATION CENTER

Atlases, almanacs, a whole set of encyclopedias? Are these really necessary when the answer to virtually any question can be found on the Internet? Many school librarians ask themselves this question when trying to stretch their book budgets to meet the needs of their school community.

Yes, print resources can seem outdated, especially when information changes so quickly, but there is merit in keeping them around. First, having learners examine the print versions helps differentiate them. It can be easy for learners to group all resources found online in the same category. How many learners answer "Google" when asked where they found their information? Second, classroom educators often request a resources lesson to prepare learners for English/language arts standardized tests. One or two lessons, no matter how thorough, won't have as big an impact as a center that learners can visit and revisit. Finally, learners actually enjoy looking through these books, especially if given the freedom to explore on their own. Encyclopedias are similar to the hugely popular Guinness World Records series, and almanacs are chock-full of quirky facts.

Providing an overview lesson before introducing this center is helpful. However, it's important to give learners enough time to explore all the resources at their own pace before asking them to answer questions. Depending on the amount of time available, this activity could easily be continued in another session. Consider allowing learners to rotate through this center, perhaps alternating it with the Database Exploration center, over a series of weeks.

If your print encyclopedias are out of date, they can still be used and can help highlight the fact that just because something's in a book doesn't mean it's still true. Be sure to explain the difference between print and online encyclopedias. This center focuses on print resources. If including databases as an option, ensure that laptops or tablets are available also.

Three Research Investigation Sheets (WS 6.9A–WS 6.9C) present some basic research questions. A blank template (WS 6.9D) is provided to customize your questions.

Objective
To explore different resources and use them to answer questions.

AASL Standards Framework for Learners
IV.A. (Curate/Think): Learners act on an information need by:
1. Determining the need to gather information.
2. Identifying possible sources of information.
3. Making critical choices about information sources to use.

V.A. (Explore/Think): Learners develop and satisfy personal curiosity by:

    1. Reading widely and deeply in multiple formats and write and create for a variety of purposes.

    3. Engaging in inquiry-based processes for personal growth.

Content Area

- English/Language Arts

Lesson Duration

20–45 minutes

Materials

- Resource Investigation Learner Directions (WS 6.8)
- Resource Investigation Sheet (WS 6.9A–WS 6.9D)
- Print almanacs, atlases, dictionaries, thesauri, and a full set of encyclopedias
- Laptops or tablets (optional)
- Pencils

Educator Preparation

1. Copy and laminate the Resource Investigation Learner Directions (WS 6.8) on card stock.
2. Make several copies of each Resource Investigation Sheet (WS 6.9A–WS 6.9C).
3. Use and copy the blank Resource Investigation Sheet (WS 6.9D) if you are writing original research questions.
4. Gather print materials.
5. Introduce the center.

Learner Steps

Individual

1. Learners look through the resources to become familiar with each.
2. Next, learners are directed to read the first question, think about which book they would use to find the answer, and circle the resource type.
3. Then learners look through that book to find the answer. If successful, they write the answer in the appropriate box. If not, they are told to repeat the process with a different resource, continuing until they find the answer.
4. Learners circle where they found the answer and repeat steps 2–4 for the second question.
5. When finished, learners compare their answers with those of a partner.

Modifications

This center is better suited to grade 2 and up. Learners who need more support can benefit from the following:

- Using a simple dictionary with pictures.
- Referring to an alphabet chart.
- Working with a partner.

Distance Learning

This activity can be used during distance learning if learners use online resources. Post the Resource Investigation Learner Directions (WS 6.8) and the Resource Investigation Sheets (WS 6.9A–WS 6.9D) online. You can post one at a time or allow learners to select from all the sheets. You should create an instructional video or step-by-step direction sheet to guide learners in accessing databases and other digital resources.

Extensions

More advanced learners can be challenged to

- create new resource questions, and
- compare and contrast print and digital encyclopedias.

RESOURCE INVESTIGATION LEARNER DIRECTIONS

Task: To explore different resources and use them to answer questions.

Steps

1. Look through the resources to become familiar with each.
2. Write your name and class on the Resource Investigation Sheet (WS 6.9A–WS 6.9D).
3. Read the first question, think about which book you would use to find the answer, and circle the resource type. You might find the same information in different books. You can use the text box to help you. Do not look for the answer yet!
4. Now, look through the book you circled to find the answer. If you find it, write the answer in the appropriate box. If you can't find the answer in the first resource, try using a different one.
5. Continue this process until you find the answer.
6. Then, circle where you found the answer.
7. Repeat steps 3–6 with the second question.
8. When finished, compare your answers with those of a partner. Did you use the same resources?

Almanac. Data, statistics, and facts about specific subjects published each year

Atlas. Maps and geographical information

Dictionary. Word definitions, parts of speech, origin, synonyms

Encyclopedia. Information about a variety of topics, usually divided into several volumes or books in alphabetical order

Thesaurus. Synonyms

RESOURCE INVESTIGATION SHEET

Name _____   Class _____

Question	Circle where you think you will find the answer.
Where was Harriet Tubman born?	almanac atlas dictionary encyclopedia thesaurus
Answer	**Circle where you found the answer.**
	almanac atlas dictionary encyclopedia thesaurus
Question	**Circle where you think you will find the answer.**
What is the capital of Estonia?	almanac atlas dictionary encyclopedia thesaurus
Answer	**Circle where you found the answer.**
	almanac atlas dictionary encyclopedia thesaurus

RESOURCE INVESTIGATION SHEET

Name _____ Class _____

Question	Circle where you think you will find the answer.
What is a synonym for brave?	almanac atlas dictionary encyclopedia thesaurus
Answer	**Circle where you found the answer.**
	almanac atlas dictionary encyclopedia thesaurus
Question	Circle where you think you will find the answer.
What is the population (number of people) of India?	almanac atlas dictionary encyclopedia thesaurus
Answer	**Circle where you found the answer.**
	almanac atlas dictionary encyclopedia thesaurus

RESOURCE INVESTIGATION SHEET

Name _____   Class _____

Question	Circle where you think you will find the answer.
What is the definition of hearty?	almanac atlas dictionary encyclopedia thesaurus
Answer	**Circle where you found the answer.**
	almanac atlas dictionary encyclopedia thesaurus
Question	**Circle where you think you will find the answer.**
Who was the fourth president of the United States of America?	almanac atlas dictionary encyclopedia thesaurus
Answer	**Circle where you found the answer.**
	almanac atlas dictionary encyclopedia thesaurus

RESOURCE INVESTIGATION SHEET

Name _____   Class _____

Question	Circle where you think you will find the answer.
	almanac
	atlas
	dictionary
	encyclopedia
	thesaurus
Answer	Circle where you found the answer.
	almanac
	atlas
	dictionary
	encyclopedia
	thesaurus
Question	Circle where you think you will find the answer.
	almanac
	atlas
	dictionary
	encyclopedia
	thesaurus
Answer	Circle where you found the answer.
	almanac
	atlas
	dictionary
	encyclopedia
	thesaurus

GEOGRAPHY CENTER

The Internet may have brought the global community closer together, but the average learner's knowledge of geography is still pretty poor. This reality can have social studies educators wringing their hands. GPS, Siri, and Waze may have negated the need for map reading skills, but technology is imperfect and not always available. Being able to use a map is important whether it's on a cell phone or in a map book. Creating and using maps are still parts of most social studies classes.

In this center, learners gain practice in fine motor skills, spatial thinking, and using resources. First, learners assemble a map puzzle (world or U.S.). Then they use the puzzle and an atlas to answer geography questions. Wooden puzzles are more durable than cardboard. Choose ones that separate the states and continents into different pieces. If purchasing duplicate puzzles, label each set by writing the same number or letter on the back of each piece. For example, if there are two identical world map puzzles, write *A* on the back of each piece for one and *B* for the other. Store the pieces in separate clearly marked plastic baggies (gallon size with a zipper works best). An inexpensive alternative is to create your own puzzles using laminated card stock maps.

Consider introducing this center by reviewing cardinal directions and how to read a map. Use the Geography Sheet (WS 6.13) to tailor questions to specific social studies content for different grades.

Objective
To complete a map puzzle and use it with an atlas to answer geography questions.

AASL Standards Framework for Learners
I.B.1. (Inquire/Create): Learners engage with new knowledge by following a process that includes using evidence to investigate questions.

IV.A.2. (Curate/Think): Learners act on an information need by identifying possible sources of information.

Content Areas
- English/Language Arts
- Social Studies

Lesson Duration
15–30 minutes

Materials

- Geography Learner Directions (WS 6.10)
- Geography World Map Sheet (WS 6.11)
- Geography U.S. Map Sheet (WS 6.12)
- Geography Sheet (WS 6.13)
- Geography Answer Sheet (WS 6.14)
- World map puzzle
- U.S. map puzzle
- World atlas
- Plastic baggies
- Ruler (optional)
- Pencils

Educator Preparation

1. Copy and laminate the Geography Learner Directions (WS 6.10) and the Geography Answer Sheet (WS 6.14).
2. Make several copies of the Geography World Map Sheet (WS 6.11) and the Geography U.S. Map Sheet (WS 6.12).
3. Use the Geography Sheet (WS 6.13) to add your own questions. Create a corresponding answer sheet.
4. Gather materials.
5. Introduce the center and review any geography skills and terms necessary.

 TROUBLESHOOTING

Some puzzle pieces may eventually be lost. The puzzle can still be used, but tell learners about the missing piece(s) beforehand. Add one or more geography questions related to the missing mystery piece. For example, if the state of Kentucky is lost, ask learners to figure out which state is missing. They can use the atlas for reference.

Learner Steps

Individual

1. Learners select a map puzzle and assemble it.
2. Next, learners choose the appropriate Geography Sheet (WS 6.11–WS 6.13) and answer the questions using the puzzle and an atlas for reference.

Partner

Learners who choose to work with a partner in this center should ensure that the work is shared equally and discuss their answers to the questions.

Modifications

Some learners might only be able to finish assembling the puzzle due to language or time limitations.

Distance Learning

Some databases and websites have geography games. These games can be used instead of puzzles during online learning. Suggestions include "Geography Explorer" on Britannica School Elementary (learners identify places on maps), the "Jigsaw" games on PebbleGo (learners assemble digital map puzzles), and the "Countries and Continents" sorting game in World Book Kids (learners drop country basketballs into the appropriate continent net). Post the Geography World Map Sheet (WS 6.11) and the Geography U.S. Map Sheet (WS 6.12) along with a link to an online atlas for learners to refer to when answering questions.

Extensions

More-advanced learners can be challenged to write geography questions to be used in the future. Upper elementary and middle school learners can work on math skills using scale and proportion to calculate distances.

GEOGRAPHY LEARNER DIRECTIONS

Task: To complete a map puzzle and use with an atlas to answer geography questions.

Steps
1. Select a puzzle to complete.
2. Work through the puzzle piece by piece until finished. You can look at maps from the atlas to help you.
3. Write your name on the appropriate Geography Sheet (WS 6.11–WS 6.13).
4. Read each question. Use the map puzzle and the atlas to help find the answers.
5. Then, write your answers on the sheet.

Tips
- Use the table of contents in the front or the index in the back of the atlas to help you find specific places.
- Hold the atlas as you would most books and check the compass rose on the map that shows directions. North is usually at the top of the page and south at the bottom. East is usually to the right and west to the left.
- Read all map keys so you understand the symbols.
- Look at the map scale and use a ruler when answering questions about distance.

GEOGRAPHY WORLD MAP SHEET

Name _____   Class _____

Use the puzzle and the atlas to answer the following questions.

Question	Answer
What is the longest river in South America?	
What is the capital of Tanzania?	
What is the largest country in Europe?	
Laos is part of which continent?	
Which country is directly southeast of Australia?	

GEOGRAPHY U.S. MAP SHEET

Name   Class

Use the puzzle and the atlas to answer the following questions.

Question	Answer
What is the capital of Montana?	
Which mountain range starts in Maine and ends in Georgia?	
How many U.S. states border (or touch) the Gulf of Mexico?	
Which desert is in parts of California and Nevada?	
Which state is due north of Wyoming?	

WORKSHEET 6.13

GEOGRAPHY SHEET

Name _____ Class _____

Use the puzzle and the atlas to answer the following questions.

Question	Answer

GEOGRAPHY ANSWER SHEET

World Map Questions

Question	Answer
What is the longest river in South America?	Amazon River
What is the capital of Tanzania?	Dodoma
What is the largest country in Europe?	Russia
Laos is part of which continent?	Asia
Which country is directly southeast of Australia?	New Zealand

U.S. Map Questions

Question	Answer
What is the capital of Montana?	Helena
Which mountain range starts in Maine and ends in Georgia?	Appalachian
How many U.S. states border (or touch) the Gulf of Mexico?	5: Texas, Louisiana, Mississippi, Alabama, and Florida
Which desert is in parts of California and Nevada?	Mojave
Which state is due north of Wyoming?	Montana

CHAPTER 7

Interdisciplinary Centers

ost people have a junk drawer, a place for all those objects that don't seem to fit anywhere else. Although useful and necessary, they defy the KonMari Method. This chapter is the junk drawer of the book because the centers included here don't fit neatly into any of the previous chapters. They're all interdisciplinary, so they're grouped together.

Most of the centers in this chapter—Mystery Box, Breakout Box, and Book Sort Geometry—are collaborative and multipart. Not only is Collaborate one of the six Shared Foundations, collaboration is also embedded in all the Shared Foundations through the Share Domain. This integration highlights the importance of collaboration. The more opportunities learners have to practice collaboration skills, the better. Consider modeling what good collaboration looks like and sounds like. Posting a reminder chart would also be helpful. Don't assume that learners, even older ones, will automatically know how to collaborate. Taking turns, listening actively, sharing ideas, and offering constructive criticism may need to be directly taught.

Each of the interdisciplinary centers targets multiple AASL Standards and content-area standards. Pretty efficient! These centers also don't require any big purchases. Most use discarded books and magazines and basic office supplies, so these centers can be implemented immediately.

ABSTRACT COLLAGE CENTER

Abstract words, which are often subjective, can be hard to define. Two people may disagree about whether a joke is funny or a pet is cute. Abstract words, like abstract art, are open to interpretation.

In this center learners define abstract words according to their own preferences. They choose a template and create a collage by cutting pictures and words from discarded magazines. Theme templates include Brave, Cool, Cute, Funny, Happy, Strong, and Unique. A blank template is also included so learners can choose their own word. This center holds the appeal of cutting and pasting, which seem to be universally beloved by learners.

Introduce the center with a discussion of the terms *abstract* and *collage,* perhaps showing examples of abstract art and collage. The variety of templates means that learners can revisit this center without replicating the activity. Although the finished products make a great display, learners usually want to keep them.

Objective
To create a collage using words and pictures to explain an abstract concept.

AASL Standards Framework for Learners
I.B.3. (Inquire/Create): Learners engage with new knowledge by following a process that includes generating products that illustrate learning.
V.A.1. (Explore/Think): Learners develop and satisfy personal curiosity by reading widely and deeply in multiple formats and write and create for a variety of purposes.

Content Areas
- Art
- English/Language Arts

Lesson Duration
10–30 minutes

Materials
- Abstract Collage Learner Directions (WS 7.1)
- Abstract Collage Template: Blank (WS 7.2A)
- Abstract Collage Template: Brave (WS 7.2B)
- Abstract Collage Template: Cool (WS 7.2C)
- Abstract Collage Template: Cute (WS 7.2D)
- Abstract Collage Template: Funny (WS 7.2E)
- Abstract Collage Template: Happy (WS 7.2F)

- Abstract Collage Template: Strong (WS 7.2G)
- Abstract Collage Template: Unique (WS 7.2H)
- Discarded magazines (many different ones)
- Scissors
- Crayons, colored pencils, or markers
- Glue
- Pencils

Educator Preparation

1. Copy and laminate the Abstract Collage Learner Directions (WS 7.1).
2. Make several copies of each Abstract Collage Template (WS 7.2A–WS 7.2H).
3. Gather all other materials.
4. Introduce the center.

Learner Steps

Individual

1. Learners choose an Abstract Collage Template (WS 7.2A–WS 7.2H) and think about the abstract term.
2. Next, learners look through discarded magazines to find and cut out words and images that will help define, explain, or depict their abstract word.
3. Learners are directed to arrange the words and pictures into a collage. They can choose any pattern but should consider how the visual format can enhance the meaning.
4. Learners make any necessary changes before gluing.
5. Finally, learners should share their collage with a classmate and then clean up.

Modifications

Consider translating the abstract terms for English learners.

Distance Learning

Post the Abstract Collage Learner Directions (WS 7.1) online and list suggested abstract words. Learners can use a blank sheet of paper, so they won't need to print the templates. With adult permission, learners can cut images and words from newspapers, magazines, or old books. They may add their own words and drawings. Encourage learners to share their creations in a safe forum online.

Extensions

Advanced learners can be challenged to list synonyms of the abstract word on the back of their template.

ABSTRACT COLLAGE LEARNER DIRECTIONS

> **Abstract.** An idea or word that cannot be defined using the senses
> **Collage.** An art process that involves cutting, layering, and pasting pieces of paper onto another paper or canvas

Task: To create a collage using words and pictures to explain an abstract concept.

Steps

1. Choose an Abstract Collage Template. You can use the Abstract Collage Template: Blank if you want to create your own. Remember, you must use an abstract word. Check with your school librarian if you need help.

2. Look through magazines to find words and pictures that explain or define your abstract word. For example, if your word is *Happy,* choose words and pictures that look happy to you or make you feel happy.

3. When you find a word or picture you want to use, cut it out. Be careful and try to cut out only your picture so other learners can use that page later.

4. Continue until you've found most or all of the words and images you want to use.

5. Arrange the clippings in a way that will help explain your theme. Move them around until you're pleased with the result.

6. Next, begin gluing each clipping to the template, layering when possible.

7. Look at the page. Do you need to add anything? If so, repeat steps 2–6 until finished.

8. Share your Abstract Collage with a classmate and then clean up.

ABSTRACT COLLAGE TEMPLATE: BLANK

Name _____   Class _____

Theme: _____

Use the area below to create your collage. Can you arrange the images to help explain your abstract theme?

ABSTRACT COLLAGE TEMPLATE: BRAVE

Name _____   Class _____

Use the area below to create your collage. Can you arrange the images to help
explain your abstract theme?

ABSTRACT COLLAGE TEMPLATE: COOL

Name _____   Class _____

Use the area below to create your collage. Can you arrange the images to help explain your abstract theme?

ABSTRACT COLLAGE TEMPLATE: CUTE

Name _____   Class _____

Use the area below to create your collage. Can you arrange the images to help explain your abstract theme?

WORKSHEET 7.2E

ABSTRACT COLLAGE TEMPLATE: FUNNY

Name _____   Class _____

Use the area below to create your collage. Can you arrange the images to help explain your abstract theme?

ABSTRACT COLLAGE TEMPLATE: HAPPY

Name _____ Class _____

Use the area below to create your collage. Can you arrange the images to help explain your abstract theme?

ABSTRACT COLLAGE TEMPLATE: STRONG

Name _____   Class _____

Use the area below to create your collage. Can you arrange the images to help explain your abstract theme?

ABSTRACT COLLAGE TEMPLATE: UNIQUE

Name _____ Class _____

Use the area below to create your collage. Can you arrange the images to help explain your abstract theme?

MYSTERY BOX CENTER

Who doesn't like a mystery? Reality food shows like *Chopped* and *Master Chef* use a mystery basket or box in their challenges. Competitors are surprised with a random assortment of ingredients and tasked with creating a tasty dish.

In this center, learners also face a mystery box of random objects. Their challenge won't end with an original meal, but they will be asked to think critically and creatively. This center can be an individual or partner activity, but working with others is preferable. Learners collaborate to find similarities among objects in their mystery box. They must find two objects at a time that have something in common (color, size, shape, material, function, etc.) and list the objects on the front of the Mystery Box Sheet (WS 7.4). Next, learners are challenged to find a similarity among as many of the objects as possible.

This center focuses as much on oral and written communication as on finding similarities. Be sure to encourage good collaboration skills, such as actively and respectfully sharing and listening to ideas.

When setting up this center, include at least ten different objects, making sure that the objects share some obvious similarities such as color, shape, or material. Change the objects frequently or have multiple mystery boxes that you rotate. These options are helpful if you're trying to quarantine materials between classes.

Objective

To collaborate and communicate with partners to find similarities among objects.

AASL Standards Framework for Learners

I.A.2. (Inquire/Think): Learners display curiosity and initiative by recalling prior and background knowledge as context for new meaning.

II.B. (Include/Create): Learners adjust their awareness of the global learning community by:

1. Interacting with learners who reflect a range of perspectives.
2. Evaluating a variety of perspectives during learning activities.
3. Representing diverse perspectives during learning activities.

Content Area

- English/Language Arts

Lesson Duration

15–30 minutes

Materials

- Mystery Box Learner Directions (WS 7.3)
- Mystery Box Sheet (WS 7.4)
- Objects
- Box or container
- Pencils

Educator Preparation

1. Copy the Mystery Box Learner Directions (WS 7.3) on card stock and laminate if possible.
2. Make several double-sided copies of the Mystery Box Sheet (WS 7.4).
3. Find a box or container to store items.
4. Gather a variety of objects (at least 10–12) for learners to examine. Make sure the objects have some obvious similarities (color, material, size, shape, purpose, etc.).
5. Consider and include necessary modifications and extensions.

Learner Steps

Individual

1. Learners take all the objects out of the box and lay them on the table.
2. Learners should take some time to examine the objects before writing.
3. Learners are asked to think about how the objects feel, what they look like, and how they're used.
4. Next, learners will find two objects that are the same in some way (color, shape, size, material, use, texture, etc.) and list them on the Mystery Box Sheet (WS 7.4) including how they are similar.
5. Learners will repeat step 4 three times.
6. As a final challenge, learners are tasked with finding a similarity among as many objects as possible and recording this on the Mystery Box Sheet (WS 7.4).

Partner

When learners work with a partner or in small groups, the steps unfold in the same order as above, except learners will discuss their ideas after step 3 and before recording their answers. Decide in advance whether each learner will complete an individual sheet or learners will use one sheet per group.

Modifications

Students who need extra support, such as English learners, learners with special education status, or younger learners with limited writing abilities, may benefit from the following scaffolds:

- Provide an example on the sheet by selecting two items and listing a similarity they share.
- Cards that list characteristics (different colors, shapes, etc.), with visuals when possible, can be provided to guide learners. For example, if given a "red" card, learners would look for two objects that are red.
- Word banks matching pictures with objects can be included for reference.

Distance Learning

Assemble 10–12 different objects on a table and photograph them together or individually. Ensure that the images are clear and close up. Post the Mystery Box Learner Directions (WS 7.3) and the Mystery Box Sheet (WS 7.4) online. Learners can share their answers with the school librarian or classmates online. This activity would also work well during synchronous whole-class instruction.

Extensions

Advanced learners can be challenged with the following additions or substitutions:
- Learners can find similarities among three objects at a time.
- Ask learners to focus on nonphysical similarities, moving beyond basic qualities such as color and shape.
- Pose these questions for learners to answer in writing: If you found all these items in a bag, what would they tell you about the owner of the bag? What might that person be using the items for?

MYSTERY BOX LEARNER DIRECTIONS

Task: To collaborate and communicate with partners to find similarities among objects.

Individual	Partner
1. Take all the objects out of the box and lay them on the table in front of you.	1. Take all the objects out of the box and lay them on the table in front of you.
2. Take a quiet moment to look at the objects and pick them up.	2. Take a quiet moment to look at the objects and pick them up.
3. Think about how the objects feel. What do they look like? How are they used?	3. Think about how the objects feel. What do they look like? How are they used?
4. Find two objects that are the same in some way (color, shape, size, material, use, texture, etc.) and list them on the front of the Mystery Box Sheet (WS 7.4).	4. Share your ideas with your partner(s) and listen to their ideas.
5. Then, write one way in which these objects are the same.	5. Find two objects that are the same in some way (color, shape, size, material, use, texture, etc.) and list them on the front of the Mystery Box Sheet (WS 7.4).
6. Repeat steps 2–5 three times.	6. Then, write one way in which these objects are the same.
7. As a final challenge, try to find a similarity among as many objects as possible. Write this on the back of the sheet.	7. Repeat steps 2–6 three times.
	8. As a final challenge, try to find a similarity among as many objects as possible. Write this on the back of the sheet.

WORKSHEET 7.4

MYSTERY BOX SHEET

Name _____   Class _____

Follow the steps from the Mystery Box Learner Directions (WS 7.3). Write your answers below.

Items	Similarities (1 per box)
1. 2.	
1. 2.	
1. 2.	
1. 2.	

(cont'd)

MYSTERY BOX SHEET

Try to find one similarity among as many items as possible.

Items	Similarity

BREAKOUT BOX CENTER

The popularity of escape rooms is undeniable. They've popped up all over the country. It's exciting to solve challenges in a group and ultimately win your freedom. The book, *Escape from Mr. Lemoncello's Library,* by Chris Grabenstein includes a similar scenario in which students are locked in the new library for a night and have to solve different puzzles to escape.

The Breakout Box center draws on these concepts. Learners must work together to complete a series of challenges. After each task is completed successfully, learners are given the code or combination to a lock. Including two to three tasks with locks is optimal for most time limits. Using more than one lock also helps build excitement.

The key to Breakout Box success is to pitch the tasks at the right level of challenge. Too easy and it's boring. Too hard and it's frustrating. For this reason, it's difficult to provide ready-made tasks for multiple grade levels and subjects. Four Breakout Box Challenges—English/Language Arts, Mathematics, Science, and Social Studies—are provided as examples. These content-area challenges are best suited for grades 3–6. They may be too easy for older learners and too difficult for younger ones. Each set of challenges has three parts that can be separated. If time is limited, use only one or two of the parts. If the group correctly solves at least one challenge by the end of class, consider giving them the codes to all the locks so they can break out. This final step is often the most fun.

A Breakout Box Challenge Planning Sheet (WS 7.10) is included for the school librarian to create grade-level– and content-area–specific challenges, perhaps in collaboration with a classroom educator. Such collaboration has several benefits: additional time means that learners can complete more parts and work at their own pace; competition among groups adds to the excitement; and challenges are targeted and timely to reinforce content-area lessons.

The Breakout Box concept is highly flexible. It can be adapted to suit various grades, content, and time limits. These concepts can also be used in a digital format, which would be useful during distance learning. Breakout Boxes can be used as a whole-class activity, perhaps to review content. Multiple sets of materials would be needed for this option.

This center does require an initial investment. Each Breakout Box set should include a box that can be locked with a hasp and exterior locks. An inexpensive plastic toolbox works well, but adding several heavy locks will make it top-heavy. See the Helpful Hints text box for more ideas about materials and logistics.

Objective

To collaborate and complete a series of tasks to open a Breakout Box.

AASL Standards Framework for Learners

I.A.2. (Inquire/Think): Learners display curiosity and initiative by recalling prior and background knowledge as context for new meaning.

II.C. (Include/Share): Learners exhibit empathy with and tolerance for diverse ideas by:
1. Engaging in informed conversation and active debate.
2. Contributing to discussions in which multiple viewpoints on a topic are expressed.

III.A.2. (Collaborate/Think): Learners identify collaborative opportunities by developing new understandings through engagement in a learning group.

III.D. (Collaborate/Grow): Learners actively participate with others in learning situations by:
1. Actively contributing to group discussions.
2. Recognizing learning as a social responsibility.

Content Areas
- English/Language Arts
- Mathematics
- Science
- Social Studies

Lesson Duration
20–45 minutes

Materials
- Breakout Box Learner Directions (WS 7.5)
- Breakout Box Challenge: English/Language Arts (WS 7.6A)
- Breakout Box Genre Cards (WS 7.6B)
- Breakout Box Answer Key: English/Language Arts (WS 7.6C)
- Breakout Box Challenge: Math (WS 7.7A)
- Breakout Box Call Number Cards (WS 7.7B)
- Breakout Box Answer Key: Math (WS 7.7C)
- Breakout Box Challenge: Science (WS 7.8A)
- Breakout Box Moon Phase Cards (WS 7.8B)
- Breakout Box Answer Key: Science (WS 7.8C)
- Breakout Box Challenge: Social Studies (WS 7.9A)
- Breakout Box Ancient Civilization Cards (WS 7.9B)
- Breakout Box Answer Key: Social Studies (WS 7.9C)
- Breakout Box Challenge Planning Sheet (WS 7.10)
- Breakout Box Parking Lot (WS 7.11)

- Breakout Box Congratulations! Sign (WS 7.12)
- Plastic or metal toolboxes with room for a lock (1 per group)
- Letter combination locks (1 per group)
- 3- or 4-digit combination locks (1 per group)
- Locks with a key (1 per group)
- Hasps (1 per group)
- Large brown envelopes
- Plastic baggies (optional to sort task materials)
- Colored paper matching lock colors
- Discarded books (1 per group with a hollowed-out compartment to hide a key)
- Calculator and other task-specific materials (optional)
- Pencils

Educator Preparation

1. Copy and laminate the Breakout Box Learner Directions (WS 7.5) and each Breakout Box Answer Sheet (WS 7.6C, WS 7.7C, WS 7.8C, WS 7.9C).
2. Make double-sided copies of each Breakout Box Challenge (WS 7.6A, WS 7.7A, WS 7.8A, WS 7.9A). Learners will write on these.
3. Copy and laminate the Breakout Box Genre Cards (WS 7.6B), Breakout Box Call Number Cards (WS 7.7B), Breakout Box Moon Phase Cards (WS 7.8B), and Breakout Box Ancient Civilization Cards (WS 7.9B). Then cut to separate and store in plastic baggies.
4. Copy and laminate a Breakout Box Parking Lot (WS 7.11) for each group.
5. Make one copy of the Breakout Box Congratulations! Sign (WS 7.12) for each box.
6. Purchase all materials and assemble the Breakout Boxes. See the accompanying Helpful Hints text box.
7. Consider and prepare any needed modifications.

Learner Steps

Partner

1. Learners read the Breakout Box Learner Directions (WS 7.5).
2. Next, they follow all task-specific instructions, completing one Challenge at a time.
3. When finished with a task, learners ask the school librarian to check their answers.
4. If the answers are correct, learners are given the code to that lock. If an answer is incorrect, learners must fix the mistake before receiving the code.
5. Learners use the code to open the lock and then place the lock on the Breakout Box Parking Lot (WS 7.11).

6. Learners continue this process until all tasks are completed and all locks are open.
7. At the end, learners must return the center to its original state.

★ **HELPFUL HINTS**

- Copy a set of all sheets for each group.
- Purchasing three different types of locks in three different colors helps when organizing tasks. Match the paper color for directions and other materials for each task with the appropriate lock. For example, if the lock for the second task is green, print the cards on green paper.
- If using multiple Breakout Box sets, number each corresponding box, lock, hasp, and envelope with the same number.
- Give all similar combination locks the same combination. (For example, all the green letter locks have READ as the combination.)
- Ensure that learners put the locks on the Parking Lot sheet once opened. This requirement prevents learners from playing with and possibly changing the combination. Put the Parking Lot on a separate table to further ensure lock safety.
- If creating your own challenges, time how long it takes to complete the task yourself. It often takes much more or less time than anticipated.
- When planning a new challenge, include a task that requires learners to move around if possible. Be creative! One task could involve singing, dancing, or other forms of dramatic interpretation.
- Use a discarded book to hide the key to the last lock. Hollow out a space inside by tracing a rectangle larger than the key on a page near the middle of the book. Cut this out. Trace the same size rectangle on the following pages and cut out until you have a space big enough to fit the key while the book is closed completely. Reshelve the book before learners arrive. The final step in the challenge is to find the book on the shelf.
- In addition to the Congratulations! Sign, consider adding other prizes to the box, such as bookmarks, to make breaking out more thrilling.
- If the answers are incorrect, do not tell learners which part needs to be fixed. This increases the challenge.

Modifications

The school librarian can support struggling learners by

- grouping learners heterogeneously for built-in assistance,
- grouping English learners with someone who can translate for them,
- providing a place value chart to use with the Breakout Box Challenge: Math (WS 7.7A),
- shortening the call numbers used for the Breakout Box Challenge: Math (WS 7.7A) and changing the place value for the rounding task in Challenge 2,
- adapting the tasks by adding pictures or word banks with key vocabulary,
- allowing learners to use calculators,
- providing content-area books or online resources for reference,
- limiting the number of tasks to one or two, and
- creating hint cards that learners can request if stuck.

Distance Learning

Numerous websites offer ready-made digital Breakout Box Challenges as well as directions on how to create your own. Google even has a Digital Breakout Template Form that you can use with Google Docs and that includes tutorials. You can take the challenge questions from this center and modify them as needed to fit the digital format.

Extensions

Advanced learners can be tasked with creating new Breakout Box Challenges.

BREAKOUT BOX LEARNER DIRECTIONS

Do you have what it takes to solve the clues and break out?

Task: To collaborate and complete a series of tasks to open a Breakout Box.

Steps

1. Read all directions first.
2. Complete the tasks in order. Do not start the next Challenge until you've opened the previous lock.
3. Work with your team to complete each task. Listen and share your ideas. Do not ask other teams for help.
4. Double-check your answers before asking the school librarian to check them.
5. If you are correct, use the code to open the lock.
6. Put the lock in the correct place on the Parking Lot worksheet.
7. If incorrect, repeat steps 3–5 until correct.
8. Put any reusable materials away before moving on to the next task.
9. Continue this process until all tasks are completed and all locks are open.
10. After you've opened the box, put everything back the way it was at the beginning.

BREAKOUT BOX CHALLENGE: ENGLISH/LANGUAGE ARTS

Name _____   Class _____

This challenge focuses on *genre,* different types or categories of books.

Challenge 1: Genre Match

1. Take the genre cards out of the bag and spread them on the table so everyone in the group can see them.
2. Read each card and then match it to its definition.
3. Each group member should check the answers.
4. Ask the school librarian to check the answers.
5. If correct, use the code to open the first lock.

Challenge 2: Finding Books

1. Find a book in the library that matches each genre.
2. Bring the books back to the table and match them with the appropriate genre cards.
3. Each group member should check the answers.
4. Ask the school librarian to check the answers.
5. If correct, use the code to open the second lock.

Challenge 3: Word Scramble

1. The genres have been scrambled! Unscramble the letters of each word below and write the correct genre next to it.
2. Each group member should check the answers.
3. Ask the school librarian to check the answers.
4. If correct, use the code to open the third lock and break out!

Scrambled Genres

1. tya freila
2. doryveyeb
3. flonts chioriatici
4. safytna
5. griboyhap
6. yeprot
7. symerty
8. oonfintnic
9. vigclap horne
10. nioster citifalic

BREAKOUT BOX GENRE CARDS

Cut out and separate the cards.

Fairy Tale	A traditional, fictional story that usually includes magical events or creatures. Princesses appear in many of these stories, which often begin with "Once upon a time."
Everybody	These are sometimes called Picture books or Easy books because they usually include illustrations and have fewer words on a page than novels.
Mystery	These books usually have a crime or puzzle that needs to be solved, often by a detective.
Historical Fiction	These stories include real, famous people and events in a made-up story.
Realistic Fiction	These stories have made-up characters and events that seem like they could be real.

Biography	These books tell about someone's life, usually a famous person, often in narrative form.
Poetry	These books are written in verse, using lines and stanzas instead of sentences and paragraphs.
Graphic Novel	These books use cartoon- or comic-style pictures with captions.
Fantasy	These stories include strange, often magical characters, settings, and events.
Nonfiction	These books include facts about specific subjects.

BREAKOUT BOX ANSWER SHEET: ENGLISH/LANGUAGE ARTS

> **For School Librarian Use:** Do not give this answer sheet to learners because they need to correct any mistakes before receiving each lock code. Use the Code spaces to write in the codes.

Challenge 1: Genre Match

Fairy Tale	A traditional, fictional story that usually includes magical events or creatures. Princesses appear in many of these stories, which often begin with "Once upon a time."
Everybody	These are sometimes called Picture books or Easy books because they usually include illustrations and have fewer words on a page than novels.
Mystery	These books usually have a crime or puzzle that needs to be solved, often by a detective.
Historical Fiction	These books usually have a crime or puzzle that needs to be solved, often by a detective.
Realistic Fiction	These stories have made-up characters and events that seem like they could be real.
Biography	These books tell about someone's life, usually a famous person, often in narrative form.

Poetry	These books are written in verse, using lines and stanzas instead of sentences and paragraphs.
Graphic Novel	These books use cartoon- or comic-style pictures with captions.
Fantasy	These stories include strange, often magical characters, settings, and events.
Nonfiction	These books include facts about specific subjects.

Code: _____

Challenge 2: Finding Books

Answers will vary.

Code: _____

Challenge 3: Word Scramble

Scrambled Genres

1. tya freila **fairy tale**
2. doryveyeb **everybody**
3. flonts chioriatici **historical fiction**
4. safytna **fantasy**
5. griboyhap **biography**

6. yeprot **poetry**
7. symerty **mystery**
8. oonfintnic **nonfiction**
9. vigclap horne **graphic novel**
10. nioster citifalic **realistic fiction**

Code: _____

(If using a key hidden in a book, give learners the call number after they complete Challenge 3.)

BREAKOUT BOX CHALLENGE: MATH

Name _____ Class _____

This challenge focuses on *decimals, fractions,* and *rounding numbers.*

Challenge 1: Decimal Order

1. Take the call number cards out of the bag and spread them on the table so everyone in the group can see them.
2. Look at each card and then put them in order from least to greatest (horizontally left to right).
3. Each group member should check the answers.
4. Ask the school librarian to check the answers.
5. If correct, find the cards that have this symbol (*) on them.
6. You will need to search the library shelves to find books that match these exact call numbers and bring them back to your table.
7. Ask the school librarian to check the answers.
8. If correct, use the code to open the first lock.

Challenge 2: Rounding Numbers and Adding

1. Look at the call numbers in the table.
2. Round each number to the nearest tenth and write the answer in the blank space.
3. Add all the rounded numbers together and write the total in the blank space.
4. Ask the school librarian to check the answers.
5. If correct, use the code to open the second lock.

Call Number	Rounded to the Nearest Tenth
811.6	
599.638	
811.008	
796.092	
975.556	

Call Number	Rounded to the Nearest Tenth
599	
796	
973.2	
398.21	
641.512	
TOTAL	

Challenge 3: Fractions

1. Look at the original call numbers.
2. How many numbers are greater than 600? Write the answer. _____
3. Now write your answer as a fraction. _____
4. How many numbers are less than 600? Write the answer. _____
5. Now write your answer as a fraction. _____
6. Which number is greater? _____
7. When finished, ask the school librarian to check your answers.
8. If correct, use the code to open the third lock and break out!

BREAKOUT BOX CALL NUMBER CARDS

Cut out and separate the cards for learners to use. Using card stock and laminating will make the cards more durable.

811.6*	599*
599.638	796*
811.008	973.2
796.092	398.21
975.556	641.512

BREAKOUT BOX ANSWER SHEET: MATH

For School Librarian Use: Do not give this answer sheet to learners because they need to correct any mistakes before receiving each lock code. Use the Code spaces to write in the codes.

Challenge 1: Decimal Order

398.21; 599; 599.638; 641.512; 796; 796.092; 811.008; 811.6; 973.2; 975.556
Code: _____

Challenge 2: Rounding Numbers and Adding

Code: _____

Call Number	Rounded to the Nearest Tenth
811.6	811.6
599.638	599.6
811.008	811.0
796.092	796.1
975.556	975.6
599	599.0
796	796.0
973.2	973.2
398.21	398.2
641.512	641.5
Total	7401.8

Challenge 3: Fractions

1. How many numbers are greater than 600? Write the answer. **7**
2. Now write your answer as a fraction. **7/10**
3. How many numbers are less than 600? Write the answer. **3**
4. Now write your answer as a fraction. **3/10**
5. Which number is greater? **7/10**

Code: _____
(If using a key hidden in a book, give learners the call number after they complete Challenge 3.)

BREAKOUT BOX CHALLENGE: SCIENCE

Name _____   Class _____

This challenge focuses on *moon phases*, *animal habitats*, and *weather*.

Challenge 1: Moon Phases

1. Take the Moon Phase Cards out and spread them on the table so everyone in the group can see them.
2. Put the moon phases in order from left to right starting with **New Moon**.
3. Match the correct moon phase name with its picture.
4. Each group member should check the answers.
5. Ask the school librarian to check the answers.
6. If correct, use the code to open the first lock.

Challenge 2: Animal Habitats

1. Match the animal with its *habitat* (where it lives) by writing each animal's letter after the habitat where it lives (for example, **Desert M**). They are not in order.

Habitat	Animal
Arctic/Tundra	A. Deer
Deciduous Forest	B. Alligator
Desert	C. Polar Bear
Grassland	D. Scorpion
Wetland	E. Dolphin
Ocean	F. King Cobra
Rain Forest	G. Zebra

2. Find a book in the library about one of the habitats or animals listed in the chart and bring the book back to your table.
3. Each group member should check the answers.
4. Ask the school librarian to check the answers.
5. If correct, use the code to open the second lock.

Challenge 3: Weather

1. Some natural disasters are caused by weather whereas others are not. Look at the following list of natural disasters and decide which ones are weather related. You may use books from the library to help you.
2. Next, each member of your group should choose one of the weather-related natural disasters to mimic or demonstrate using sounds and movement.
3. All members of your group should practice their performance before showing the school librarian.

Natural Disasters

- Blizzard
- Earthquake
- Flood
- Hurricane
- Tornado
- Tsunami
- Volcanic eruption

1. After each performance, tell the school librarian which natural disaster was portrayed.
2. If everyone is correct, use the code to open the third lock and break out!

BREAKOUT BOX MOON PHASE CARDS

Cut out and separate the cards.

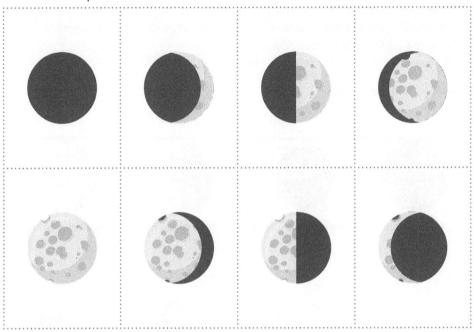

new moon	**waxing crescent**	**first quarter**	**waxing gibbous**
full moon	**waning gibbous**	**third quarter**	**waning crescent**

BREAKOUT BOX ANSWER SHEET: SCIENCE

> **For School Librarian Use:** Do not give this answer sheet to learners because they need to correct any mistakes before receiving each lock code. Use the Code spaces to write in the codes.

Challenge 1: Moon Phases

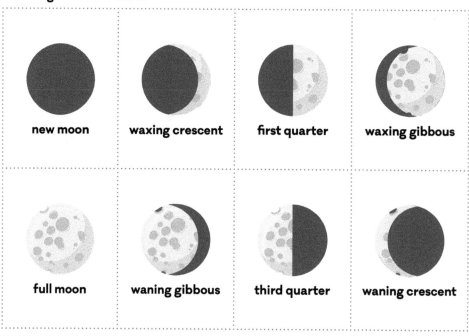

new moon	**waxing crescent**	**first quarter**	**waxing gibbous**
full moon	**waning gibbous**	**third quarter**	**waning crescent**

Code: _____

Challenge 2: Animal Habitats

Habitat	Animal
Arctic/Tundra C	A. Deer
Deciduous Forest A	B. Alligator
Desert D	C. Polar Bear
Grassland G	D. Scorpion
Wetland B	E. Dolphin
Ocean E	F. King Cobra
Rain Forest F	G. Zebra

Book choices will vary.

Code: _____

Challenge 3: Weather

Weather-Related Natural Disasters

- Blizzard
- Flood
- Hurricane
- Tornado

Code: _____

(If using a key hidden in a book, give learners the call number after they complete Challenge 3.)

BREAKOUT BOX CHALLENGE: SOCIAL STUDIES

Name _____   Class _____

This challenge focuses on *geography*, *ancient civilizations*, and the *American Revolution*.

Challenge 1: Geography

1. List the continents and oceans in alphabetical order.

	Continents		Oceans
1		1	
2		2	
3		3	
4		4	
5		5	
6			
7			

2. Label the continents and oceans on the blank map.

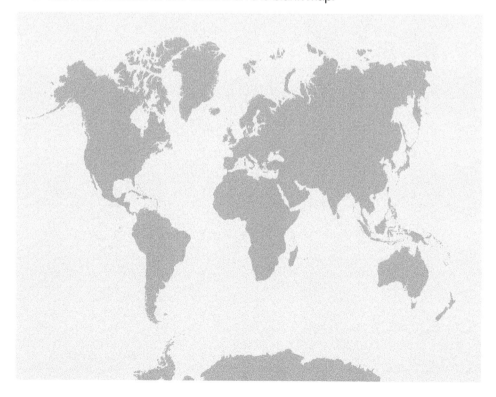

3. Each group member should check the answers.

4. Ask the school librarian to check the answers.

5. If correct, use the code to open the first lock.

Challenge 2: Ancient Civilizations

1. Take the Ancient Civilization Cards out and spread them on the table so everyone in the group can see them.

2. Place the heading cards (Ancient China, etc.) in a horizontal row.

3. Look at each invention card and discuss which ancient civilization first created the item shown. Place each card under the appropriate heading.

4. Each group member should check the answers.

5. Ask the school librarian to check the answers.

6. If correct, use the code to open the second lock.

Challenge 3: American Revolution

1. You may use books or the Internet to help you answer these questions.

    a. Who signed the Declaration of Independence first?

    _____

    b. What year was the Declaration of Independence written? _____

    c. Who became the first U.S. president? _____

    d. Who was the first U.S. vice president? _____

    e. Which Virginian said, "Give me liberty or give me death!" in a speech?

    _____

    f. Who ruled Great Britain during the American Revolution?

    _____

    g. How many colonies were there during the Revolutionary War? _____

    h. Which Founding Father invented bifocals and the lightning rod?

    _____

    i. What year did the Revolutionary War end? _____

    j. Who famously rode his horse through the Boston area to warn patriots that the British soldiers were coming? _____

2. Find a biography of one of the people listed in question 1 in the library and bring the book back to the table.

3. Each group member should check the answers.

4. Ask the school librarian to check the answers.

5. If correct, use the code to open the third lock and break out!

BREAKOUT BOX ANCIENT CIVILIZATION CARDS

Cut out and separate the cards.

Ancient China	**Ancient Egypt**
Ancient Greece	**Ancient Rome**
Hieroglyphics	**Wheelbarrow**
Aqueducts	**Pyramids**
Doric Columns	**Olympics**
Silk	**Paper (from papyrus)**
Democracy	**Fireworks**
Kites	**Roman numerals**

BREAKOUT BOX ANSWER SHEET: SOCIAL STUDIES

> **For School Librarian Use:** Do not give this answer sheet to learners because they need to correct any mistakes before receiving each lock code. Use the Code spaces to write in the codes.

Challenge 1: Geography

1. Continents and oceans in alphabetical order

	Continents		Oceans
1	Africa	1	Arctic
2	Antarctica	2	Atlantic
3	Asia	3	Indian
4	Australia	4	Pacific
5	Europe	5	Southern
6	North America		
7	South America		

2. World map filled in

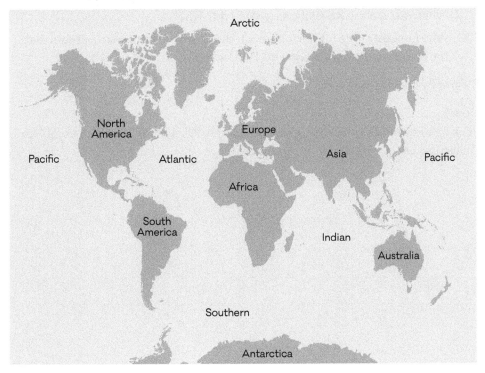

Code: _____

Challenge 2: Ancient Civilizations

Ancient China	Ancient Egypt	Ancient Greece	Ancient Rome
Wheelbarrow	Hieroglyphics	Olympics	Roman Numerals
Silk	Pyramids	Doric Columns	Aqueducts
Fireworks	Paper (from papyrus)	Democracy	
Kites			

Code: _____

Challenge 3: American Revolution

1. Who signed the Declaration of Independence first? John Hancock
2. What year was the Declaration of Independence written? 1776
3. Who became the first U.S. president? George Washington
4. Who was the first U.S. vice president? John Adams
5. Which Virginian said, "Give me liberty or give me death!" in a speech? Patrick Henry
6. Who ruled Great Britain during the American Revolution? King George III
7. How many colonies were there during the Revolutionary War? 13
8. Which Founding Father invented bifocals and the lightning rod? Benjamin Franklin
9. What year did the Revolutionary War end? 1783
10. Who famously rode his horse through the Boston area to warn patriots that the British soldiers were coming? Paul Revere

Biography choices may vary.

Code: _____

(If using a key hidden in a book, give learners the call number after they complete Challenge 3.)

BREAKOUT BOX CHALLENGE PLANNING SHEET

When creating a new Breakout Box Challenge, consider content-area standards as well as AASL Standards. Use the following template to help you plan. Retype the template on another page using the previous Breakout Box Challenges (WS 7.6A–WS 7.9A) for reference. Don't forget to make an answer sheet for yourself.

Content Area	
Standards	
Number of Tasks/ Locks and Codes	
Challenge 1	
Challenge 2	
Challenge 3	

BREAKOUT BOX PARKING LOT

Put each open lock in the correct box.

Lock 1

Lock 2

Lock 3

Lock 4

BREAKOUT BOX CONGRATULATIONS! SIGN

Congratulations!
YOU BROKE OUT.

BOOK SORT GEOMETRY CENTER

Will that new couch fit through the doorway? How much carpet or paint will you need for that home improvement project? The ability to accurately measure something is an essential life skill. This is why measurement is taught early in the primary grades. Learners often wonder, "Why do I need to know this?" Any adult knows that math concepts such as addition, multiplication, measurement, area, perimeter, and volume will be used throughout a person's life.

In the Book Sort Geometry center, learners practice these important math skills after sorting books into different categories. This collaborative center starts with a pile of discarded books. Learners examine the books and discuss ways to sort them, ensuring that each group member participates. Then learners sort the books into different categories and explain their rationale in writing before repeating the process once more. Next, they measure the length and width of each book and record the dimensions.

Younger learners may need a demonstration of how to measure. Perimeter and area are usually not taught until fourth grade, so primary grades will most likely stop there. Older and more-advanced learners will continue and compute perimeter, area, and possibly volume. Provide formulas if needed.

Objective
To collaborate when sorting books into different categories and solving math problems.

AASL Standards Framework for Learners
II.A.1. (Include/Think): Learners contribute a balanced perspective when participating in a learning community by articulating an awareness of the contributions of a range of learners.

V.C. (Explore/Share): Learners engage with the learning community by:
    2. Co-constructing innovative means of investigation.
    3. Collaboratively identifying innovative solutions to a challenge or problem.

Content Areas
- English/Language Arts
- Mathematics

Lesson Duration
20–45 minutes

Materials
- Book Sort Geometry Learner Directions (WS 7.13)
- Discarded books of varied sizes and genres (at least 10 per group)
- Math formulas (optional)
- Calculators (optional)
- Rulers (1–2 per group)
- Pencils

Educator Preparation
1. Make several copies of the Book Sort Geometry Learner Directions (WS 7.13).
2. Gather all materials.
3. Number the books 1–10 (or 12 if using more books).
4. Review basic measurement and math concepts with learners if needed.

Learner Steps

Partner
1. Learners spread the books in front of them with the covers facing up. They look at the books and think about possible ways to sort them.
2. Next, learners discuss their ideas with their group and listen to others' ideas.
3. Learners agree on categories and sort the books.
4. After the books are sorted, learners describe the categories on the Book Sort Geometry Learner Directions worksheet (WS 7.13).
5. Learners repeat steps 2–4.
6. Then, learners take turns using rulers to measure the length and width of each book and record the dimensions on the Book Sort Geometry Learner Directions worksheet (WS 7.13).
7. Finally, learners use these data to calculate the perimeter and area of each book and record the results.

Modifications
The school librarian can support struggling learners by
- suggesting categories for learners to choose from, such as fiction and nonfiction or size, and
- providing math formulas and calculators.

Extensions
Advanced learners can be given the following challenges:
- Measure in inches and centimeters.
- Compute the volume of each book.
- Compare and contrast the books using proportion.

BOOK SORT GEOMETRY LEARNER DIRECTIONS

Name _____   Class _____

Task: To collaborate when sorting books into different categories and solving math problems.

Steps

1. Spread out the books in front of you with the covers facing up. Then, look at the books and think about possible ways to sort them.

2. Discuss your ideas with your group and listen to others' ideas until you agree on how to sort the books.

3. Now, sort the books into different categories.

4. Describe how you sorted them.

   _____

   _____

5. Now, sort the books another way and describe it below.

   _____

   _____

6. Measure the length of each book in inches and record the results below.

1.	6.
2.	7.
3.	8.
4.	9.
5.	10.

7. Measure the width of each book in inches and record the results below.

1.	6.
2.	7.
3.	8.
4.	9.
5.	10.

8. Subtract the length of the smallest book from the length of the largest book. What is the difference? (Use a separate scrap paper to calculate the math problems.)

9. Find the perimeter (P) and area (A) of each book and record the results below.

1. P =   A =

2. P =   A =

3. P =   A =

4. P =   A =

5. P =   A =

6. P   A =

7. P =   A =

8. P =   A =

9. P =   A =

10. P =   A =

CONCLUSION
Some Final Advice

Now that you've read the book, you know what learning centers are and why you should use them. It's my hope that you've now got everything you need to set up learning centers in your own school library. A word of advice—instead of jumping in with both feet and introducing several new centers at once, start small. Maybe just dip your toe in the first week by focusing on one or two centers that you feel really comfortable with. Continue to introduce new centers each week. There is no right or wrong way to use learning centers. Take the ideas in this book and adapt them to fit your school library and learners. You may even be inspired to create some learning centers of your own.

Most school librarians have a similar goal: to foster a warm, welcoming environment in which learners are engaged, challenged, and nurtured. If learners have positive experiences in the school library early on, they are more likely to become lifelong library patrons. Learning centers are one way to build that positive association. They can help make your school library a place that learners are excited to visit again and again. Good luck!

APPENDIX A
Other Center Suggestions

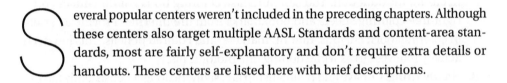everal popular centers weren't included in the preceding chapters. Although these centers also target multiple AASL Standards and content-area standards, most are fairly self-explanatory and don't require extra details or handouts. These centers are listed here with brief descriptions.

1. **Board Games:** Video games seem to have replaced traditional board games as entertainment, so many learners may have little experience with them. Board games can help teach important skills such as taking turns, following rules, and practicing good sportsmanship. Inexpensive games that can be finished in a short time include Boggle, Scattergories, Matching, Connect 4, backgammon, and Spot it.

2. **3-D Pens:** School librarians who have makerspaces may have considered purchasing a 3-D printer. The cool factor is undeniable, but these printers have several drawbacks for use in a center. They're expensive, they can be difficult to use, and they are often very time-consuming. Alternatively, 3-D pens offer a similar product but let the learner take a more active role. The pens are much less expensive, are easier to use, and offer instant results. Learners follow directions to create various items or can draw freestyle to create their own designs.

3. **Origami:** Origami is hugely popular with elementary school learners, so this center will certainly attract visitors. It's also super easy to set up. All you need are some origami books or directions and paper. If you don't want to take any origami books out of circulation, you can download simple step-by-step instructions and laminate them for learners to use. Buy a box of origami paper or use pages cut to size from discarded books and magazines.

4. **More Technology:** There are so many free and exciting apps and websites for learners to explore. You can set up some tablets or laptops and allow learners to choose from a curated list. Choose apps and websites that do not require separate accounts, such as Sock Puppets and LEGO Movie Maker. Check out AASL's Best Apps and Websites for Teaching and Learning for other great sites such as PBS KIDS ScratchJr and ChatterPix Kids.

5. **Alphabet:** This center is great for beginning readers. All you need are upper- and lowercase magnetic letters and a metal cookie sheet or magnetic board. Learners can put magnetic letters in order, match upper- and lowercase letters, and form words.

6. **Magnetic Poetry:** This center can be used for learners to write poetry, sentences, or even paragraphs. You need a set of magnetic words, ideally color coded by part of speech, and a metal cookie sheet or magnetic board. Learners create a poem or sentence and can take a picture or copy it down to preserve and share it.

7. **Coloring:** This is a perennial classic that is inexpensive, is easy to set up, and needs no introduction. You can purchase coloring books or download copyright-free coloring sheets and bookmarks from the Internet. Provide a variety of coloring tools: crayons, fine-tip markers, and colored pencils. This low-tech activity relieves stress while honing fine motor skills.

8. **Handwriting:** Cursive and penmanship are, sadly, no longer consistently taught. As a result, many students have poor penmanship. Yes, computers are great, but so is legible handwriting. Because learners don't often get this instruction in class (really, where's the time when you've got state tests to prepare for?), this center would be fun and easy for those just learning to write and for older learners. Provide different types of pens and paper. Also, consider adding books on calligraphy, hieroglyphics, or Morse code.

9. **Project Review:** Create a center in which learners can watch and respond to the videos and book reviews made in other centers: Mini Green Screen, Book Trailer, Video Book Review, LEGO Story, and Book Spine Poetry.

10. **Magnify It:** This center can include old-school magnifying glasses and microscopes or cool tech gadgets like the Zoomy digital microscope that connects to a computer. Include a variety of objects for learners to examine.

Learning Center Labels

Copy and cut out the following learning center titles and use them to label storage containers or direction folders.

Abstract Collage Center

Blackout Poetry Center

Book Cart Center

Book Sort Geometry Center

Book Spine Poetry Center

Book Trailer Center

Breakout Box Center

Construction Center

Database Exploration Center

Endangered Books Center

Fairy-Tale Challenge Center

Geography Center

Grammar Hunt Center

Innovation Station Center

LEGO Story Center

Maker Challenge Center

Matchbox Car Engineering Center

Mini-anagram Center

Mini Green Screen Center

Mystery Box Center

Photo-Book Center

Resource Investigation Center

Simple Machines Center

Video Book Review Center

Word Drawing Center

INDEX

CPSIA information can be obtained
at www.ICGtesting.com
Printed in the USA
LVHW011057200422
716157LV00002B/5